grow your own
vegetables
in containers

grow your own
vegetables
in containers

deborah schneebeli-morrell

CICO BOOKS
LONDON NEW YORK

This edition published 2009 for Index Books Ltd

Published in 2009 by CICO Books
an imprint of Ryland Peters & Small Ltd
20–21 Jockey's Fields, London WC1R 4BW

www.cicobooks.co.uk

10 9 8 7 6 5 4 3 2

Text copyright © Deborah Schneebeli-Morrell 2009
Design and photography copyright © CICO Books
2009

A CIP catalogue record for this book is available
from the British Library.

ISBN-13: 978-1-906525-99-6

Printed in China

Project Editor: Gillian Haslam
Text Editor: Henrietta Heald
Designers: Roger Hammond and Roger Daniels
Photographer: Heini Schneebeli
Illustrator: Jane Smith

Dedication
To my dear friend Jehane Markham, a pioneer
of organic food and a thoughtful gardener.

Author's acknowledgements
Thanks to all my friends, gardeners, vegetable
growers and allotment holders who shared their
gardening knowledge and who allowed us to
photograph in their 'plots'. In particular, Mick Rand,
Bill Saunders, Chris Jackson, Alan and Anthea
Stewart, Helen Scott Lidgett, Jill Patchett and
Gloria Nicol.

I am indebted to Heini Schneebeli for his
perseverance and skill in photographing the
projects in the book during a particularly poor
summer for veg growers.

I would like to thank John Levis of Bygones at
Whitehall Garden Centre in Lacock Wiltshire for
lending some props and recommend a visit to his
outdoor shop for inspiration and a source of lovely
vintage domestic and garden objects.

Contents

Introduction

Increasing concern about climate change has made us more conscious of where our food comes from and how it is produced. We know about the unwelcome effects of industrial-scale farming and the negative influence that humans have had on the environment. Sustainability and green issues are at the forefront of many people's minds, and there is a general desire to live healthier lives while lessening our impact on the planet.

We have learned that it is better to eat seasonal vegetables that are locally grown rather than those that have been flown thousands of miles around the world to reach our shops and markets. As a result, more and more of us are 'growing our own'. One great advantage of this is that it allows us to harvest crops minutes before eating or cooking them – and really understand the meaning of the word 'fresh'.

Vegetables deteriorate very quickly after they are picked because the natural sugars start to turn to starch, and by the time commercially grown vegetables reach the shops the flavour is already greatly diminished. That is why frozen peas (which are frozen immediately after harvest) are superior in flavour to so-called fresh peas, which may not reach the shops until a day or two later. Don't just take my word for it. When you start to grow your own vegetables, do a little experiment. Pick and eat a lettuce or carrot or whatever you grow and then eat a shop-bought version, and you will have your proof – there's no comparison.

Pesticide residues, which are still found in commercially grown vegetables, can be harmful to human health, so if you want to be sure that your produce is pesticide-free, you need to cultivate it yourself. Shop-bought organic vegetables are relatively expensive – another good reason to grow your own.

Gardeners who grow their own produce are doing real work – the kind of work that originated with our ancient farming ancestors.

Left: *Chillies come in so many different varieties and are well suited to being planted in colourful empty olive-oil cans.*

Right: *Borlotti beans quickly climb up tall canes, producing a heavy crop of speckled red pods. These are left to ripen on the vine and are harvested by opening the dried pods.*

Given such a long history, you might be discouraged by the thought that there is too much to learn, too much tradition to absorb, but this knowledge is widely spread and many people are happy to share their experience, whether by word of mouth or through books and manuals.

Above: *This old, sturdy, wire potato harvesting basket makes a useful container for growing tomatoes.*

It is a fact of nature that plants will grow. Your role is to help to create the right conditions to encourage and enhance that process.

Urban gardening

There is a widespread trend among city-dwellers to grow vegetables in the smallest spaces – on windowsills and balconies, in patios and back yards. Unlike many fashions, this one is really welcome. It represents a movement away from the processed and the packaged, away from mass production and shopping – and, importantly, it challenges the domination of supermarket culture. Do we really need particular vegetables and fruit to be available all through the year? Does a strawberry at Christmas, grown in a huge industrial greenhouse, bear any relation to an indigenous one grown in the open air and ripened by the sun? Do we want to buy a little packet of clingfilm-wrapped French beans cultivated in a far-off place and sprayed many times? And do we want to pay high prices for these dubious fruit and vegetables?

More and more people are saying no to these questions. Among them are those of us who do not have much outside space but want to grow our own and enjoy some of the advantages that were traditionally gained from gardening on a vegetable plot or in a larger garden. This is easier than it sounds; many vegetables are adaptable and can be grown in reasonably compact containers.

Tomatoes, perhaps the most adaptable crop, have long been cultivated in the ubiquitous growbag, often perched on a small balcony or even a windowsill. With its flat-sausage shape and garish plastic skin, a growbag is an ugly object; it is also difficult

to water – and all sorts of even uglier gadgets have been designed as growbag accessories to help watering and to help prop up the tomato vine. The best way to treat a growbag is to cut it open and use the compost in a more attractive container.

Gardening for children

If you have children, encourage them to become involved in cultivating the produce they will eventually eat. This will teach them where and how food is grown, and they will

Above: *Chard will grow well in a roomy window box on a sunny windowsill, and adding an attractive shell mulch will help to retain moisture in the compost.*

come to realize that treating the earth with care and respect can bring delicious fresh rewards. Sowing seeds and watching them germinate and thrive is a real pleasure, and this small world of growth, harvest and renewal that you have created will connect you and your family to the vast ecosystem of nature.

Gardening organically

Gardening organically is about working with nature. It is not a scientific process; it is just common sense – and has long been practised by thoughtful gardeners. If you are growing all your vegetables in pots in a small space, it is not easy to be completely organic since this would involve making your own compost to feed and enrich the soil. However, if you follow the famous adage 'feed the soil not the plants', you will be well on the way to creating healthy, sturdy, pest-resistant plants. Where possible, buy organic compost.

If you have enough space, do create a compost heap – as well as reducing the amount of organic waste going to landfill, this will give you a continuous supply of rich compost to add to the soil that you will doubtless have to buy in. Avoid pesticides since these kill beneficial insects as well as those that may be devouring your crops. In reality, greenfly are wonderful food for garden birds and for ladybird and hoverfly larvae; slugs are loved by frogs and toads; and snails are a delicacy for the songthrush – you may have been lucky enough to hear a songthrush

Above: *Adding freshly cut comfrey to your compost adds a boost of useful nutrients and encourages good cropping of your vegetables.*

tapping a snail shell on an 'anvil' stone to reveal the nutritious flesh inside. An organic gardener values and protects these creatures. Feed your crops occasionally, especially while they are producing fruit. Use a natural fertilizer such as seaweed extract or homemade comfrey liquid (see page 16).

The organic method includes companion planting: pairing vegetables with flowering plants that encourage beneficial insects and predators as well as plants with a scent that repels other potential pests (see page 29). It really is a logical system.

Left: *As well as the flowers, bees will pollinate your vegetables.*

Right: *Bees love borage flowers for the rich, sweet nectar they produce. Borage is an annual and grows quickly into a sturdy plant covered in clear blue star-like flowers.*

getting started

The art of gardening and growing food crops is neither mysterious nor difficult. Before shops and increased urban living, many people, out of necessity and tradition, managed to grow a few staple crops in order to feed their family.

We still have the same needs; perhaps we are not so poor but many of us would like to grow at least some healthy crops to supplement our family diet, and so gardening, particularly vegetable growing, is becoming extremely popular. Gardeners are very generous people and so you will not have to look far to find help and advice, and a huge range of books and gardening magazines is available from which you can glean much useful information.

If you are intending to grow a few vegetables in containers in a small urban space, it's not difficult to get started. You won't need many tools – a small trowel and fork will be useful, as will a dibber for making holes in the compost in which to plant seeds and transplanted seedlings.

A few sacks of general-purpose compost are essential (peat-free and organic is best), and a bag of well-rotted manure is useful to enrich the soil for hungry crops, such as beans and courgettes.

The nicest task will be finding, re-using and recycling suitable containers and you will find inspiration on the following pages. Some of the projects use mulches to retain the moisture. As well as being practical, these can be decorative, and using shells or pebbles collected on holiday will bring back happy memories.

Sowing seed and caring for young seedlings is exciting, and you will learn most by doing it yourself. If necessary, follow the advice to use a plastic storage box as a coldframe in the absence of a greenhouse.

Don't worry too much about pests and diseases. These are usually made out to be worse than they are, and your plants will be healthy if you try to be as organic as you can.

Choosing containers

The choice of containers is endless. If you use your imagination and invention to recycle items you already have, you will not only devise interesting planters but also add striking decorative touches to your outside space. Outside space is now often considered an extension of inside space. Just as you might choose a piece of furniture, a vase or a picture to enhance an interior, you will also want to choose pots and other containers to make your exterior space interesting and beautiful.

Once you start looking, you will find all sorts of objects – some discarded, rescued or borrowed – that can be adapted or converted to make containers for growing produce. Traditional terracotta pots are lovely, but you may prefer the colourful decorative qualities of empty olive-oil cans, for example. If colour is your thing, consider acquiring some brightly coloured plastic garden trugs. Old baskets can

Above left: Coloured, rubber, all-purpose tubs make brilliant, practical and decorative planters.

Above: This roomy supermarket basket has been planted with spinach, holding enough compost to ensure a healthy crop.

be lined with plastic to conserve moisture; galvanized buckets and baths or wooden wine or fruit boxes are among many other options.

The planting projects in this book use a wide variety of containers, each of which has been carefully chosen to match the crop and give it the best chance of success. Some crops need less space than others. For example, quick-growing salad can be sown in a shallow container, such as a washing-up bowl or a kitchen colander, while rooted crops, including carrots, need more depth. Beans need a long root run, but radishes, being speedy croppers, can thrive in a more limited space.

Above: *Strawberries, both wild and cultivated, grow happily in old wooden fruit or wine boxes.*

Far left: *Rocket grows quickly and almost anywhere. All sorts of kitchen containers are well suited to this easy crop.*

Left: *Similarly, radishes are a quick-growing crop and will thrive in these small plastic bowls as well as looking pretty.*

Composts and soils

The most important aspect of any gardening, and the key to real success, is to make sure that your soil is fertile, well balanced in essential nutrients, and moisture retentive without being too wet. Enthusiastic beginners often become downhearted at the poor progress of their plants, not realizing that an initial investment of time, thought and research into soils and composts will provide bounteous rewards.

Start your own compost heap

If you have enough outside space, the best thing to do is to start a compost heap. There are many ready-made closed systems available, most of which consist of a large plastic container with a close-fitting lid. Among the benefits of a compost heap is a reduction in the amount of waste that needs to be collected from your home. Above all, you will have a rich compost full of beneficial organisms, including worms, to add to your bought-in soil. For those with less space, a smaller 'wormery' is ideal. This consists of a large colony of worms, which devour and convert your vegetable scraps into much sought-after wormcast, a particularly fine and fertile compost.

Potting compost

Don't use homemade compost or pure wormcast for sowing. Vegetable seeds need a sterile soil with no weed seeds or pathogens that might damage the young seedlings. Poor compost can cause 'damping off', in which the base of the new stem rots and the previously healthy seedling flops over and dies.

It is advisable to buy a special seed compost, which will contain a limited quantity of nutrients and fertilizer – you don't want the

comfrey liquid

Very rich in nutrients, comfrey liquid is believed to have almost magical properties. It is easy to make yourself. Comfrey is a common plant that grows tall and dense; its flowers are much loved by bees. If you have the space, you could grow a patch specially but, if not, you may be lucky enough to find some, perhaps in a friend's garden. Cut a plant to the ground – it will quickly regrow. Chop it up and follow the instructions on page 91. Then just add a large splash to a can of water before watering. Tomatoes, peppers, courgettes and aubergines will all benefit from a weekly feed. Comfrey leaves can also be dug into compost or used to make an excellent mulch.

seedlings to romp away with a lot of lush leafy growth and little strength.

It is possible to find commercially produced organic compost for seed sowing, but check the label. Some manufacturers offer so-called organic products that would not necessarily meet organic accreditation standards. There is no need to be too rigid; just steer clear of chemically enhanced composts.

The John Innes series of soil recipes, while not organic, offers a reliably high standard. The soils are loam-based with added sand, peat and nutrients, and come in three grades: No. 1 for seed sowing; No. 2, which has more nutrients for potting on; and No. 3, the richest soil, which is designed to feed more mature plants. A general-purpose compost can be used for all three stages of growth, but the crops will need to be fed as they mature and ripen.

Peat has long been valued as a growing medium by the horticultural industry, but its use for this purpose is now strongly discouraged since the continued extraction of peat threatens the destruction of ancient peat bogs. Aim to use one of the peat substitutes, which may be made from coir, composted bark or recycled waste.

Feeding your plants

You can add well-rotted manure to a general-purpose compost to make a rich and nutritious medium in which to grow hungry plants, such as beans, peas and courgettes. It should not be used for root crops, such as carrots, however, since it will cause the roots to fork or distort. Spent mushroom compost, which contains a lot of straw, is wonderful for lightening the soil, but it is rich in lime, which doesn't suit all crops; strawberries and raspberries, for example, do not thrive in a lime-rich soil.

Above: *Courgettes are easy to grow in a large container but they do need a rich compost. Add freshly cut comfrey and mix in a little well-rotted manure or homemade compost.*

Crops grown in containers should ideally be fed a few weeks after planting to boost the fertility of the compost. There are many proprietary organic feeds available, some liquid and some that are incorporated into the surface of the compost. A weekly feed of seaweed extract or comfrey liquid (see left) is ideal.

Sowing and growing

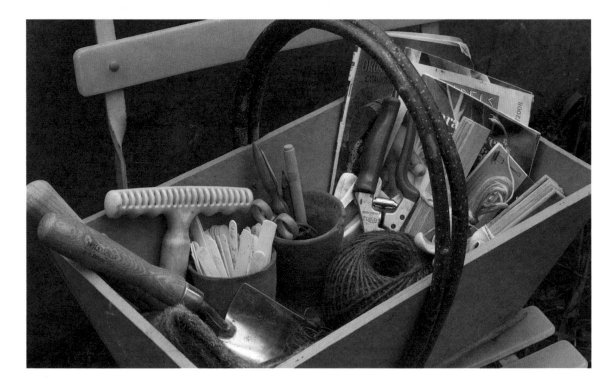

One of the gardener's winter pleasures is reading seed catalogues and planning what to grow, but deciding which lettuce, beetroot or carrot to order can be confusing. When choosing vegetables for pots, look for plants that crop quickly and are described as being suitable for container growing.

Buying and storing seeds

Organic seeds are readily available from dedicated suppliers, but you may enjoy searching through the seed packets on display at your local garden centre. Gardeners collect seed packets throughout the year in the same way that some people collect shoes. Luckily, seeds can be viable for a long time, especially if kept in cool, dry conditions out of the light. Before you buy seeds, read the text on the

Above: A small trug will be large enough to hold an assortment of tools, including a trowel and secateurs, as well as useful bits and pieces, such as string, labels and perhaps a seed catalogue.

Right: Read the seed catalogues or the back of seed packets so that you find suitable varieties.

packet, which will describe the characteristics of the plant, the conditions required for successful growing, and the planting and cropping times. Seeds can be expensive, and the amount of seed varies greatly from packet to packet. Italian packets that used to be available only in delicatessens are the least expensive and the most fully packed. The internet has opened up the market, so that gardeners are no longer limited to buying seeds from suppliers in their own country.

Growing from seed

Seeds are programmed to germinate and grow into mature plants. To thrive, they need warmth, light and moisture, as well as a sterile growing medium – never use garden soil or recycled compost because these will contain fungi and bacteria that could damage emerging seedlings. A seed-sowing compost is best; John Innes No. 1 (a loam-based compost) is ideal. Don't let seedlings dry out and never expose them to extremes of temperature.

If you are growing a small number of vegetables, you can sow them in trays or pots and let them germinate on a sunny windowsill. It is a good idea to grow tomatoes, chillies and peppers in this way because they need to be started early in the year, in a warm place, in order to have a long enough season to produce a good crop.

Most keen gardeners want a greenhouse. Apart from its practical advantages, a greenhouse can be a wonderful haven from a busy world, a place to be alone with your thoughts. It may be that you can only aspire to such a luxury, but there are many other ways of sowing seeds and nurturing seedlings. One of the most inventive is to create a mini greenhouse or cloche from a large clear-plastic storage box with a detachable lid. If this is placed in your outdoor space with the lid on, the internal temperature will be a few degrees higher than outside. Remember to ventilate the box on warm days by putting a stick under the edge of the lid; otherwise, the tender young seedlings you have planted could be damaged by a sudden build-up of heat.

Left: *Using clear plastic storage boxes as a cold frame is a good idea. With the lid in place, you will be able to increase the temperature inside the box. This is important since warmth is what makes seeds germinate.*

Above: *After you have sowed your bean seeds, you could speed up germination by covering the compost with a piece of glass. (For safety, make sure it has smooth sides.)*

All kinds of container are suitable for sowing seeds, including plastic trays, pots, cells and modules, eggboxes and even supermarket packaging. A plastic container with a lid – the sort that soft fruit is sold in – can be used as a mini cloche; such containers are usually perforated in the base and the lid, providing a convenient means of drainage and ventilation.

Clear-plastic drinks bottles can be adapted to drip-feed plants, to make a temporary cloche, or to protect vulnerable young plants against snails and slugs.

The cardboard tubes inside lavatory rolls or kitchen towels make wonderful biodegradable pots, especially for larger seeds such as peas or beans. A paper potter – a simple two-part wooden tool – makes useful little pots out of strips of newspaper (see page 25).

If you sow seeds sparingly, you will be able to minimize disturbance of the seedlings when

Left: *A cut-down plastic water bottle makes a useful collar around a young plant, protecting it from the hungry advances of slugs and snails.*

Below: *Some seeds, such as basil, seem to have 100 per cent germination, so you will need to thin them out and plant them apart so that mature plants have enough space to grow.*

thinning later. It is sometimes a good idea when sowing fine seeds, carrots in particular, to mix them with a little sand because this helps to disperse the seeds. For larger seeds, such as courgettes, peas, cucumbers or beans, sow two in each pot or cell and discard the weaker when they have both grown their first set of real leaves.

The next stage is pricking out – selecting the healthiest seedlings and replanting them, more widely spaced, in new compost (see page 16).

Hardening off is the important process that occurs between the early protected seedling growth and the permanent transfer outside of the sturdier mature plants. To achieve this successfully, leave the lid off the cloche during the daytime for a few days until the plants become adapted to cooler conditions. Eventually, when the nights are warmer and any danger of frost has passed, take off the lid or take the plants outside permanently.

Above: *Use the space around potted trees to plant a crop of salad, spring onions or rocket.*

Intercropping

Intercropping is when you plant a smaller, fast-growing crop using the space between slower-growing larger vegetables. The quick crop matures just as the slower crop begins to need more space. Typical combinations include lettuce grown around cabbages and broccoli, and radishes and spring onions grown between carrots.

Decorative standard trees are often grown in pots (olive trees are particularly popular). Rather than leaving bare soil at the base, use it to plant a salad crop – lettuces or spring onions will thrive in these conditions, and even larger onions will grow well. Rocket and radishes will be happy as well as the large variety of cut-and-come-again salads. Dig a little organic fertilizer into the compost at the top of the pot before planting your intercrop.

Buying young plants

If you don't have the time or space to grow all your vegetables from seed, you can buy young plants. Good nurseries will provide healthy ones ready to plant out. It is a sensible idea to buy tomatoes in this way because you can order a selection of different varieties to grow together. Chillies, aubergines and cucumbers are also usually available as young plants and are normally planted out from late spring, when the danger of overnight frost has passed.

Top: *You will need to buy in strawberry plants early in the season if you want them to bear fruit the same year.*

Above: *Unless you have enough space to grow chillies from seed much earlier in the season, it is best to buy in young plants. Look out for those grown organically.*

Plant support

Some plants need a structure to climb or scramble over. Peas are traditionally trained up pea sticks, cut from any branching wood such as hazel, lime, birch, alder or beech (see page 114). The height of the pea sticks will depend on the variety of pea; they vary from dwarf size to 1.8m (6ft) tall. Pole beans, or runner beans, grow very tall and need to twine around rods or canes. Dwarf French beans may need tying in to stop them flopping over the sides of the container. Beans are easier to pick if well supported.

Newspaper pots

The best kind of pots are those that can be planted directly into the soil and allowed to degrade naturally, such as the newspaper pots shown here. They cut down on work since you don't have to remove the plants from the pots, and the seedlings are healthier because their roots are not disturbed in the way they would be when potting on from a small to a large container. The green advantage to this method is that it removes the need for plastic pots.

These pots are made by wrapping folded strips of newspaper around a two-part tool called a paper potter. The potter consists of a wooden cylinder, which is pushed firmly into a wooden base – an action that folds and secures the paper to form a pot. Paper pots are ideal for planting peas and beans of all kinds because these plants have long roots that will penetrate the paper.

Above: *Tear the newspaper into strips about 10cm (4in) wide and 50cm (20in) long. Wrap a strip of newspaper around the potter a few times so that it reaches just over the cylinder at the handle. Overlap the base by about 3cm (1¼ in). As you push the cylinder firmly into the base of the potter, the paper will fold to make the bottom of the pot. Remove the cylinder from the base and carefully pull it out of the pot. Fill the pot with the compost ready for planting.*

Watering and mulching

Vigilance about watering is vital when growing plants in containers. Only a limited amount of moisture can be stored in a pot, and most pots lose water through evaporation, mainly from the surface of the compost. A potentially leaky container, such as a basket, should be lined with plastic. Don't forget to make drainage holes in the base; waterlogging is as damaging as drying out. To enhance drainage, put a layer of broken pots or crocks in the base of your container before adding the compost; stones, pebbles, grit, sharp sand and even broken polystyrene containers are suitable alternatives.

Various products are designed to aid water retention in compost; these are usually in the form of granules that swell and take up water. They must be used carefully and only in small containers. Although one or two projects in this book include water-retaining granules, I am not generally in favour of them because they alter a natural process and can lead to overwatering.

When to water?

It is preferable to check the compost regularly, looking for signs of thirst in your plants, and giving plenty of time and thought to the process of watering. Early morning or later in the evening are the best times to water. Plants can be damaged by watering in the hot sun; water droplets on a plant act like a lens, allowing the sun to burn the leaves. Too light a water at the wrong time will encourage the roots to reach for the surface and risk scorching. I regard watering as my quiet, observant, thinking time – the special time that I spend on my own with my plants.

Mulches

An effective way to counteract evaporation is to add a mulch around the base of the plants on the surface of the soil. Almost anything will do. Bark chippings make a dark covering, whereas broken china or sea shells are more decorative; comfrey leaves are nutritious as well as attractive. If you are growing strawberries, straw has the added advantage of lifting the berries off the soil and away from slugs.

Colour and tone of mulches can be important – for example, the light tone of crushed sea shells spread around the base of rainbow chard will reflect the light and speed up their growth.

Left: *Mulches are practical as well as decorative and can include crushed sea shells, pea gravel and slate pieces. These are available from garden centres and suppliers.*

Right: *The idea is to cover the exposed soil so a variety of materials will do – try straw, polished pebbles, chipped bark, china shards and terracotta crocks.*

Dealing with diseases and pests

A great fuss is made about plant diseases and pests, much of it generated by chemical companies seeking to sell products designed to deal with these problems. Commercial preparations are usually best avoided, although there are a few benign chemicals that are permitted in the organic system.

In reality, the most effective way to guard against any disease or pest is to grow sturdy, healthy plants in a well-balanced compost. Don't overcrowd your plants and allow good air circulation. Make sure they have enough light; sun is important, but don't let them overheat. Water regularly, and go easy on the feeding – never give more than the amount specified on the packet.

There is growing opposition to the use of chemicals in horticulture because of the damage they can do to the environment. The good news is that there are not many serious pests to contend with if you are cultivating vegetables in the controlled environment of a container.

Carrot root fly and flea beetle

Fortunately, these two particularly annoying pests – the carrot root fly's maggot burrows deep into the carrot, and the flea beetle nips tiny holes in radish, rocket and some oriental salads and brassicas – pose minimal risk to container-grown vegetables simply because they cannot fly above a height of 20cm (8in).

In a vegetable plot, these pests can be deterred by erecting a low barrier around the rows of plants. There are many products available on the market to protect vegetables against such pests, a light nylon mesh being the best option.

Above: *A small snail, so often the gardener's enemy, is fascinating to watch as it glides on its slime trail across a leaf. Collect them at night by torchlight.*

Slugs and snails

Slugs and snails are greedy feeders attracted by soft new growth and they can demolish a plant overnight. All gardeners hate these pests, but far too many toxic pellets are used to control them, with the result that the soil is contaminated and the poisoned carcases of the snails and slugs may be eaten by toads, thrushes or hedgehogs, with devastating consequences for those beneficial creatures.

There is an organically approved pellet made from ferrous sulphate, which breaks down in the soil, but the best method of dealing with slugs and snails is to be vigilant and pick them off plants and containers when you spot them. Slugs and snails are dormant during the day, sticking under the rims of pots or shady places out of the light. They feed at night, so a visit with a torch can result in quite a harvest. Collect them in a bucket of salt water, which will kill them quickly.

Another option is to place a mechanical barrier around a tender seedling – a plastic water bottle with the base cut away has become a standard and effective method. An extra precaution is to wrap a strip of copper around the top of a container; slugs and snails won't cross the metal.

Scooped-out grapefruit shells placed skin up around your vegetable plants make handy hiding places for slugs and snails. Simply check them each day and remove the culprits.

Aphids

Aphids, in particular greenfly and blackfly, can damage a plant by sucking the sap; the tell-tale signs are twisted or distorted leaves. The juicy bugs make nutritious food for fledgling birds, and hoverflies and ladybird larvae also rely on a healthy diet of aphids. If infestation is causing damage, a good blast of water from a hosepipe will dislodge most pests.

Cats and birds

If gardening on a patio, roof terrace or windowsill, you won't be challenged by rabbits, deer or mice, but you may be affected by cats; cats love fresh compost and may think you have provided them with a convenient cat tray. Until your plants have grown, you could use a hard mulch such as china shards or shells to deter them. Twiggy sticks inserted in the soil will also do the trick.

Birds may be a problem. In towns, pigeons can do a lot of damage; they love to peck at peas, broad beans, chard and cabbages. Blackbirds like berries of all kinds, although, curiously, raspberries seem to survive. Simple measures can have a deterrent effect. Anything that flaps or whirrs will scare them off – a child's wind wheel is ideal. Other effective deterrents include old CDs – the silver side of the disc flashes against the light – and strips of coloured plastic bag tied to a string and suspended over the plants.

Companion planting

Grow your vegetables alongside other flowering plants if you can. The companion flowers will attract pollinating insects, which will also visit your bean and tomato flowers, your courgettes, peas, chillies, peppers and aubergines. Chives or garlic alongside carrots will deter the carrot root fly, and the pungent aroma of basil or French marigolds growing near tomatoes will discourage whitefly.

The herbs savory and thyme grown around broad beans will deter infestation of blackfly. Stately fennel and borage, with its lovely star-shaped blue flowers, both invite bees and hoverflies, the two most beneficial insects in the vegetable garden.

Above: *By far the most useful and well tested companion plants are the fiery orange tagetes, with their pungent scent that deters whitefly and other aphids. They have the added bonus of having a long flowering season.*

essential herbs

Herbs can be grown successfully in the smallest of outside spaces, even a small balcony or a kitchen. As long as they have good compost, plenty of light, a fair amount of sun and warmth, most herbs will thrive in containers. If you are new to vegetable gardening, it is no bad thing to start by growing herbs. You will soon graduate to growing vegetables and then you can put your herbs and vegetables together in the kitchen to make delicious meals.

Among hardy perennial herbs that can survive at quite low temperatures are the alliums. This family includes chives, a useful everyday herb that is easy to grow and has pretty purple edible flowers. Welsh onions are similar to chives but have rather bulbous hollow leaves; and garlic chives have strap-like leaves and lovely white flowers.

Sweet majoram, oregano, savory and thyme will tolerate dry conditions. The taller, untidy tarragon needs more space, but is also worth growing – make sure you choose the French type rather than the Russian, since the latter has a rather weak flavour. Rosemary and sage are larger evergreen shrubs with a woody framework; both should be planted in generously sized pots with a good depth of compost. Many varieties of mint are also popular with gardeners – Tashkent and Moroccan mints are best for making tea.

Annual herbs, which last for one season only, should be grown from seed. Indispensable varieties include basil, dill and coriander. Annuals will flower and set seed in a season so, to extend the harvesting time, remove all the flowering shoots when they are young and tender.

Among other essential herbs are parsley and chervil. These are biennials, meaning that they flower and set seed in the second season after planting. Chervil, which grows in an appealing mound of feathery leaves, deserves to be more highly prized as a culinary herb. It will happily survive the winter and self-sow in the spring.

A basket of mixed herbs

you will need

vintage basket

plastic bag to fit inside the basket

felt hanging-basket liner

compost

water-retaining granules

herbs, such as flat-leafed parsley, thyme, lemon thyme, marjoram

bark mulch

Traditional cane baskets are still widely available and generally good value; examples from the 1950s often have a decorative strip of plastic threaded around the rim and handle. A well-loved vintage basket that is slightly worn and can no longer hold shopping securely is ripe for recycling as an original planter. It must be able to hold enough compost to create a good growing medium. You will need to line it, first with plastic to protect the natural materials in the basket, then with felt. Adding water-retaining granules will help to keep the compost moist and reduce the need for endless watering on hot days. A bark mulch also reduces evaporation from the surface of the compost.

green*care*

Thyme (lots of different varieties, but especially lemon thyme), flat-leafed parsley, marjoram and chives are all particularly well suited to container growing.

Right and far right: *You may like to buy small herb plants to pot on in a larger container, as here. They are generally inexpensive, but it can be more rewarding to grow your herbs from seed or cuttings.*

1 Push the plastic bag into the basket so that it covers the whole of the inside, coming well up the sides of the basket. Cut a few slits in the base to allow for drainage.

2 Place the felt liner on top of the plastic and push into place, trimming the edges to fit the shape of the basket if necessary.

3 Add the compost, mixing in a small amount of the water-retaining granules (follow the instructions on the packet) in the lower section of the compost.

4 Plant the herbs, placing the smaller thymes at the front and the taller parsley and marjoram at the back. Water well and cover the compost around the herbs with bark mulch.

herb hints

- Start by growing the most familiar culinary herbs. Then experiment with a few more unusual types and find new recipes that incorporate them.

- Basil is an indispensable container herb (see pages 38 and 42). Every one of the tiny black seeds will germinate. A few small basil seedlings ready to pot on make an excellent present for a keen cook.

- Chervil, my favourite, is a less well-known herb with an aniseed flavour (see page 36). It is delicious in salads and on buttered new potatoes.

- Fennel with its graceful habit and feathery leaves in green or bronze must have a deep container to accommodate its long roots.

- Bushy perennials, such as rosemary and sage, need large pots filled with a compost that is more soil-based than that used for other herbs.

- Dill, coriander and summer savory thrive in pots. To keep them healthy and productive, give them plenty of water and harvest often.

- Mints are rampant growers and need to be confined in containers (see page 45), otherwise they will quickly overgrow everything in their path. Repot mints and replenish the soil regularly to retain the herbs' depth of flavour.

Above: *Coriander is a quick-growing herb often used in Middle Eastern and Asian cooking. Pick the leaves to prevent the plant flowering (although the flowers are edible).*

Right: *The leaves of African basil may be used in cooking. They have a mellower flavour and the scent of cloves.*

Far right: *The leaves of purple sage have a delicate colour.*

Year-round chervil

Chervil is a pretty herb that deserves to be better known and more widely grown. It has delicate fernlike leaves and white umbelliferous flowers resembling those of parsley. The older leaves turn subtle shades of pink, especially in cool weather.

Chervil is widely used in French cooking, in salads, soups, sauces and omelettes. It is easy to grow sown from seed and will thrive in cool, damp conditions in partial shade. Surprisingly, chervil is winter hardy, making it one of the few herbs that can be grown throughout the year, and it has the advantage of being a vigorous self-seeder. Although you can sow the seed in spring, I find it grows better when sown from midsummer onwards.

green*care*

If you sow chervil seeds in a wet period, watch out for slugs and snails, which enjoy eating the young seedlings. See page 28 for ideas for keeping them at bay.

Far right: *A wicker basket makes a suitable container for chervil. Remember to line it with plastic to retain moisture.*

Right: *Chervil is a hardy biennial with delicate lacy leaves. It will tolerate a certain amount of shade and can withstand cold so that it may continue to grow in winter. Light and temperature affect the colouring of the leaves – the occasional pink or purple ones look lovely in a salad. For a constant supply of chervil, sow seed every few weeks from midsummer.*

Sweet basil in a clay pot

One herb I could not live without is basil. Its clove and aniseed scent is surely the most penetrating fragrance of all the herbs. A perfect partner for succulent home-grown tomatoes, it is also the key ingredient of pesto – the most exquisite sauce ever created. To make pesto, simply pound fresh basil leaves with extra-virgin olive oil and combine with crushed pine nuts, grated Parmesan cheese and chopped garlic.

Basil plants are easy to grow and will thrive inside or out as long as they are in a warm sunny position. In Mediterranean countries you will see them on windowsills and doorsteps, sometimes planted in empty olive-oil cans. Each variety has a subtly different flavour.

The most commonly grown variety, sweet basil, or *Ocimum basilicum*, is a reliable half-hardy annual, meaning that you sow the seeds each year and the plant dies down in the autumn. The blousy aromatic leaves are large and crinkled, releasing their pungent aroma at the gentlest touch. Thai basil has smaller leaves with purple undersides and is widely used in Thai sauces and curries; it has a more pronounced aniseed flavour and is always cooked. Bush basil, or Greek basil, has smaller leaves and makes a decorative compact plant. Its flavour is less intense than that of sweet basil.

greencare

Sturdy basil plants grown from seed, planted in rich compost and nurtured by the summer sun are in a different league from the sappy supermarket pots of overcrowded seedlings, which will last a few days only. Home-grown basil should last the summer. To extend its life, pick off any flowering shoots.

Right: *A generous traditional terracotta pot containing a few well-spaced plants will provide you with enough fragrant basil leaves to last the whole summer.*

1 Read the seed packet carefully and follow the sowing instructions. Fill the seed tray with the sowing compost and pat down. Sprinkle the seed thinly over the surface. Add a fine layer of compost until the seeds are covered. Water with a fine rose. Keep the seeds in a warm place, such as on a sunny windowsill, until they germinate.

2 Wash out the clay pot thoroughly and place a few large stones or broken crocks in the base to encourage good drainage.

3 Fill the pot with the mixed compost and tamp down. Use a dibber to make holes in the compost large enough to take the seedlings without squashing their roots.

4 Carefully lift the seedlings out of the seed tray, first loosening them with the dibber. Hold the seedlings by the first leaves only, to avoid squeezing or damaging the delicate stalks.

5 Space the seedlings a few centimetres apart – the plants will grow large and if there are too many they will be vying for the food in the composts. Water the seedlings well and keep them out of the hot sun for a few days until the roots become established in their new position. Water regularly and wait patiently for the plants to grow.

Right: *Purple ruffles is an extravagant variety of sweet basil that has deep purple, crinkled leaves. It is less hardy than the green variety, and its leaves are less aromatic, but they are used torn in salads to add spectacular and unusual colour.*

African basil and sage

These two bushy shrubs both grow well in containers, providing the pots are big enough to hold a good depth of compost. With African basil especially, bear in mind that the pot may have to be moved in the winter because this plant doesn't much like cold weather.

Right: *African basil is a shrubby perennial, meaning that it does not set seed or die back. It has decorative blue-tinted leaves with purple veining, and long spikes of lilac flowers, which are irresistible to bees.*

Above: *Sage, like rosemary, is an evergreen shrub from the Mediterranean area. It has a pungent flavour that goes well with liver, potatoes and squash. Varieties include a variegated sage with cream and white blotches on the furry grey leaves, purple, common and broad-leaved sage. They all bear attractive bluish-purple flowers that are very attractive to bees. Keep the bush trimmed and transfer into a larger container after a year or so if you want the plant to increase in size.*

herbs in long toms

If you are interested in food and cooking, it is essential to have a good supply of herbs within easy reach of the kitchen. The herbs chosen for these long tom pots are some of the most widely used in Mediterranean countries.

- Rosemary (seen in the large pot on the left of the photo) makes a woody evergreen shrub that can be clipped into a topiary shape. It is often added to lamb or chicken before roasting and makes a wonderful partner to garlic when added to a pan of roasting potatoes.

- There are so many varieties of thyme that it is hard to know which one to choose. A pale-leaved common thyme forms an attractive miniature shrub (seen in the large pot on the right). The smaller pot on the right contains a creeping thyme that will have pretty pink flowers. Lemon thyme, a chef's favourite, is also well worth growing. The secret with thyme plants is to keep them well trimmed and not to let them grow leggy and untidy. I like to sprinkle a few sprigs of thyme along with some sea salt and good-quality oil on a butternut squash, cut in half lengthways before baking in the oven.

- Golden majoram (seen in the small pot on the left) is a spreading bushy herb that can be cut back each spring to regenerate. Add it to beetroot and feta salad with extra virgin olive oil and fresh lemon juice.

- All these Mediterranean herbs will grow well for a year or so in the long tom pots, but, as they enlarge and want to grow into shrubby plants or bushes, they should be transplanted to larger containers. They love to grow in sun and will tolerate some drought. Plant in a loam-based compost such as John Innes No. 3.

Below: *If you are short of space, plant your herbs in long toms. Since they are tall, they hold more compost without using too much horizontal space.*

Galvanized buckets filled with mint

Above: *The pale mauve flower spires of black-stemmed mint, loved by bees, appear late in the season. Mint leaves lose some of their pungency when the plant flowers, so cut off the blooms if you want to use the leaves in cooking. Otherwise, crop strongly flavoured mints, such as spearmint and Moroccan mint, and leave other varieties to flower.*

Left: *Plant a selection of mints in vintage galvanized buckets. You just need to make a few drainage holes in the base to make a perfect planter.*

Mint is widely used medicinally (as a digestive and decongestant), in cosmetics (as a cleanser and stimulant), in the kitchen (as a flavouring) and to make teas. There are hundreds of varieties, offering many different flavours, so before growing mints for use in drinks or food, compare mature plants by rubbing the leaves between your fingers and choose the ones that have the scent you prefer. Moroccan or Tashkent mint is perfect for making a refreshing tea, while apple mint is often used to flavour the water when boiling new potatoes. Pennyroyal, a powerful, low-growing peppermint, makes a useful spreading plant along the edges of paths and patios. As you brush past or tread on the leaves, the intense aroma will fill the air. I rub it into my face and hair to stop the midges biting when I am working in the garden late in the evening.

It makes sense to grow mint in a pot sunk into the soil, which prevents the vigorous roots from overrunning nearby plants. The herb likes some shade and plenty of moisture. Mint grown in a container will do well for a year. It develops into a large plant very quickly, using up all the nutrients in the compost. This means that the intensity of the flavour will be reduced; to restore it, replenish the soil regularly each spring – or consider starting again with a new young plant.

These vintage galvanized buckets are inexpensive to buy and make ideal containers for a variety of contrasting mints. Keep them by your back door so you can easily pick a few leaves when needed.

growing mint

When you remove a young mint from its original pot ready for planting up in your own container, you will see how the roots are raring to go – they will take off as soon as they reach some lovely new compost. You will probably have to divide the vigorous plants in spring and replenish the compost. Mint can also be used as a companion plant to repel insects, but its vigorous growth means that you do need to be careful where you plant it.

Welsh onions and garlic chives

Chives, garlic chives and Welsh onions belong to the allium family, which also includes garlic and leeks. Ordinary chives may start to look rather tired as the season progresses, especially if they are grown in a container; it is worth cutting the leaves back to encourage a healthy regrowth. Garlic chives have strap-like leaves with a mild garlic flavour and are much favoured in Chinese cooking. The pretty white flowers are edible and, pleasingly enough, bloom late in the year. All in all, this is a rewarding and tidy plant that, because of its good looks, is often grown in the flower border.

Welsh onions are hardy plants that can grow quite tall. Their tubular leaves attached to a bulbous thickened base will remain green all year; they have a strong onion flavour.

green*care*

You can grow chives, garlic chives and Welsh onions from seed but, to save time, you may prefer to buy them from a nursery or garden centre as young plants. They will enlarge quickly, creating more bulbs, which will make the plant congested in the pot in time. However, alliums are easy plants to propagate. Simply divide the clumps by pulling apart the bulbs, and create several new plants by planting a group of them in a separate pot.

Left: *The fluffy white globe flowers of Welsh onions sit on top of the fat hollow stems and, like the more finely cut purple chives, can be very decorative. Use like chives.*

Right: *The flowers of garlic chives are very welcome at the end of the summer when all else is dying down. They look good planted in this unusual ribbed clay pipe. Just stand on a clay saucer or directly onto soil.*

leaves and shoots

My aim is to cut some green leaves to eat every day of the year. To achieve a year-round harvest, you need to sow seed successionally – that is, sow more of the same seed every few weeks. In winter, protect your plants from cold, wet weather by covering them with a coldframe or a cloche.

Salads are quick and fairly easy to grow. Since they are shallow-rooting, they will thrive in containers. Window boxes, washing-up bowls, buckets and all sorts of domestic containers are perfect. Plastic containers are particularly good because they allow minimal evaporation. Water your salad plants regularly in the evening, and don't let the compost dry out; prolonged drought will stunt the growth of a salad plant and produce leaves that are tough and bitter. For a colourful salad, grow a mixture of red, green, speckled, crinkly and smooth leaves – each variety has a different taste.

Another must is peppery-flavoured rocket. Both the wild variety, with its finely cut leaves, and the cultivated type, with its nutty edible flowers, are quick to germinate and grow. Oriental greens – the red-veined mustard and cut-leaved mizuna, and corn salad, also known as lamb's lettuce – do better when sown later in the summer; they seem to respond to cooler weather and shorter days. If you sow seed several times, at regular intervals, you will be able to harvest leaves until late in the year.

Chard is another leaf crop that is decorative as well as being a versatile vegetable. Grow broad white-stemmed Swiss chard or varieties with more unusual colours. Bright Lights, with its lemon-yellow, pink and white ribs, and the exotic fuchsia-pink ruby chard are quite magical.

Beetroot and carrots look wonderful when their vibrant hues contrast with a colourful container. Radishes grow well in a small container but will not thrive in hot sun. Keep them moist and cool, and sow every two weeks to ensure a constant supply.

Wild rocket in a kitchen colander

you will need

multipurpose peat-free compost

coir or felt hanging-basket liner to fit colander

water-retaining mat

aluminium colander, as wide and deep as you can find

organic rocket seeds

green*care*

Start to harvest the rocket when each plant produces a number of strong leaves. Cut them as you need them and watch them regrow. After a number of cuttings, the plant will want to flower. At this point, your second crop, sown a couple of weeks later than the first, will be reaching maturity.

Rocket is easy to grow, making it a popular crop in the vegetable garden. Quick to germinate and mature, it can be sown successively throughout the summer to ensure a continuing supply. Alternatively, sow once or twice and treat as a cut-and-come-again crop, cutting just a few leaves from each plant at a time and then leaving it to produce more.

Wild rocket has finer cut leaves and a more peppery taste than the cultivated variety. It is a perennial and can be overwintered because it is able to withstand frosts. Cultivated rocket is an annual with tender leaves and a relatively mild taste. When it eventually runs to seed, it produces beautiful cream-coloured, four-petalled flowers.

If you want a supply of rocket throughout the year, it will grow happily on a kitchen windowsill during the colder months. Keep your rocket plants well watered, especially in hot weather, when they have a tendency to bolt or run to seed. If they suffer from a lack of water, the leaves will become tough and unpleasant to eat.

The only pest that may attack rocket is the flea beetle, which bites tiny holes in the leaves. The beetle is unlikely to trouble container-grown plants as it cannot jump high enough to reach most pots, but, if it is a problem, you can cover the crop with a fine mesh or net.

When it comes to using recycled containers in your vegetable garden, aluminium kitchen pots, pans, sieves and colanders are undiscovered classics that are widely available at jumble sales, flea markets and charity shops. The old aluminium colander used here resembles a garden urn and makes an entertaining but practical container for rocket. It is large enough to hold enough compost for the crop, although a water-retaining mat has been added in the base to conserve as much moisture as possible.

Right: *This old colander makes a perfect urn-like planter for the finely cut leaves of wild rocket. You will easily find similar examples in jumble sales or junk shops. Add a few old aluminium pots and pans and you can make a real 'kitchen garden'.*

1 Put the hanging-basket liner inside the colander – you may need to cut and overlap to fit if the sides of the colander are steeper than a hanging basket.

2 Put a little compost into the base of the colander and cover it with the water-retaining mat. There's no need to cut this to fit the base of the container.

3 Fill the colander up to the rim with compost, press down firmly and sow the seeds thinly over the surface of the compost. Sprinkle a fine layer of compost over the seeds to cover them, pat down and water well with a fine rose. (It is important to use a fine rose because a jet of water would wash all the seeds to one side.)

4 Keep the compost moist at all times. When the seeds have germinated and the seedlings are growing strongly, you will need to thin them out to allow each plant sufficient space to grow. If you are very patient by nature, you could even wash all the surplus seedlings and add them to a mixed salad.

Right: *The flowers of cultivated rocket are edible, and add a nutty flavour to salads; they are superior in taste to the yellow flowers of wild rocket.*

Cut-and-come-again salad leaves

Growing cut-and-come-again salad leaves makes it possible to have fresh salad ingredients at your fingertips every day throughout the summer. For a continuous supply, you need to sow successively – that is, every couple of weeks or so. These cheap and cheerful plastic window boxes are easy to find in markets and shops.

'Cut-and-come-again' means just what it says. Instead of growing individual lettuces for harvesting as a whole, you grow a number closer together and crop individual leaves as they grow. The idea is that the plant will then grow new leaves, which can be continually cropped over a few weeks. If you sow seeds a couple of weeks apart through the season, you can extend the harvest over several months. You can even have a late crop when the weather is colder, as long as you cover the plants with a cloche or horticultural fleece.

Baby spinach leaves can also be grown as a cut-and-come-again salad crop, as can mizuna, mustard and corn salad (or lamb's lettuce). If you sow these later in the season, ideally after midsummer, they seem to do better and suffer less from problems such as bolting. Sow the seeds directly in the prepared compost and thin out when they are 2.5–5cm (1–2in) high, allowing at least 10cm (4in) between plants. You can eat the sweet-tasting thinnings in a salad or use as a garnish.

you will need

- brightly coloured plastic window boxes
- multipurpose peat-free organic compost mixed with a little loam-based compost
- seed of spinach
- seed of mixed salad leaves
- crocks made from a polystyrene planting tray, broken into small pieces

green*care*

Seed merchants sell a wide variety of cut-and-come-again salad crops and, if you sow over a season, you will be able to try out quite a few. Mixtures are attractive, often combining red and green lettuces as well as plain and curly leaves.

1 Put the broken polystyrene pieces in the base of each window box. This layer of drainage crocks should be 2.5–5cm (1–2in) deep.

2 Fill the window boxes almost up to the rim with the compost mix. Pat the surface with the palm of your hand to make it even and level.

3 Put the spinach seed in the palm of one hand and use the other to sprinkle it lightly onto the compost.

4 Gently sprinkle a light layer of compost over the seed so that it is all covered.

greencare

If you sow your seed early in the season, you can speed up germination by placing a sheet of glass or Perspex or even a large clear plastic bag over the window box. This creates a mini greenhouse and increases the soil temperature.

Right: *These brightly coloured plastic window boxes are really cheap to buy. They are light and easy to move and make a brilliant contrast to the pure green young leaves of spinach as well as the decorative curly leaves of the red lettuce. Pick the leaves when young and tender and water well. Lettuce will quickly become tough and bitter if short of water.*

5 Repeat with the other box, sowing salad leaf seed. This is much finer seed, so sprinkle it lightly. Water both boxes with a fine rose so as not to dislodge the seeds.

6 When the seedlings are 2.5–5cm (1–2in) high, thin them out to allow the remaining ones to grow sturdier. Allow 5–10cm (2–4in) between each seedling.

Red lettuce and perilla in enamel tins

When you grow vegetables in a small space, you don't want all your crops to be green. Luckily, salad vegetables come in many tones of purple and red – from radicchio, with its deep-red veins, to the vibrant magenta stems of ruby chard and the purple globes and leaves of some of the older varieties of beetroot, while the fuchsia pink of radish

flashing against a deep-brown soil is both intriguing and beautiful.

One of the richest and darkest reds is seen in the Japanese herb perilla. Its frilly, almost metallic-toned, nettle-like leaves are strikingly similar to purple basil. They are bland to taste but make a salad look very pretty. The green variety, which is used in Japanese cooking, has a much stronger taste. Sow perilla seed in spring in pots or modules and don't plant out until all risk of frost has passed.

Enamel flour and bread bins were commonly used in kitchens until late last century and can still be found in flea markets and junk shops. Often brightly coloured or printed with vintage text to describe the original contents, they make adaptable and unusual planters for everyday salad crops.

greencare

There are many varieties of red lettuce. A loose-headed type is ideal to grow in a small planter because you can cut the stem above the soil and new shoots will be produced all around the cut. Allow these to grow and keep cutting throughout the summer. Lettuces can be sown successfully from early spring until late summer to ensure a continuous supply; as long as the weather is not too cold, they will always grow. Continue to grow in a cloche or coldframe to extend the season.

As they grow quickly, lettuces can be planted in smaller containers, but they need plenty of moisture and good drainage. Give them a very dilute liquid feed every week to add nourishment to the soil.

Above left: *Loose-headed red crinkly lettuce will thrive and grow in an enamel bin, but don't stand it in continual hot sun or the tender leaves will wilt.*

Right: *Lovely vintage kitchen containers, often printed with descriptive text, are relatively easy to come by. The unusual dark lustrous leaves of the perilla mean it is grown more for decoration than for the kitchen, but it is a reliable plant.*

Salad bowls

two plastic washing-up
bowls 45cm (18in) in
diameter and 17cm (7in)
deep

organic peat-free
multipurpose compost

pea gravel

cordless electric drill

selection of salad
plants, including red and
green loose-leaf
lettuces, giant red
mustard and mizuna

purple slate as a mulch

greencare

Salads need less soil
than some crops, but
they must have enough
to stop them getting
dry or parched. A
thirsty lettuce will
become bitter and run
to seed more quickly
in dry conditions. Be
careful also not to
leave them in the hot
sun – this will make
them wilt and it may
be difficult to revive or
refresh the affected
leaves.

Even if you don't grow any other vegetables in your container garden,
do try a few salad varieties. It is possible to grow enough salads in
various containers to keep you going all through the summer and well
into the autumn. The best ones to grow are the cut-and-come-again
types – harvest a few leaves to eat and simply wait for the plant to grow
more. You can keep a crop going for some time, but it would be wise to
sow seed or plant seedlings a month later in another pot to make sure
of a continuing supply.

There are plenty of seeds available for cut-and-come-again salad
crops, but a quicker alternative is to buy some young seedlings and
plant them, correctly spaced, directly into the compost. The loose-
leaved varieties are most suitable. Green and red lettuces look good
together both in the pot and on the plate. For added taste and variety,
grow a selection of oriental salad greens. These generally do better
when planted later in the summer. Giant red mustard with its peppery
hot flavour and pretty red-veined leaves is a must in a container garden.
Combine it with the milder cut-leaved mizuna.

Large plastic washing-up bowls are ideal salad planters. They are
cheap to buy and come in a variety of colours and sizes. You will
need to make some drainage holes in the base, but there will be no
evaporation through the sides.

Right: *Two large plastic
washing-up bowls planted
with a variety of salad leaves
will be enough to provide you
with a salad every day. To
ensure a continuous supply,
plant a couple more bowls
a month or so later.*

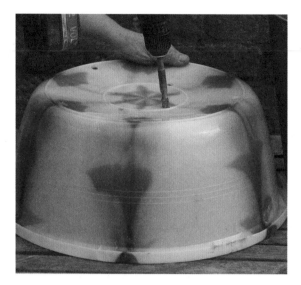

1 Turn the plastic bowl upside down, making sure that it is on a firm surface. Drill a number of holes in the base about 10cm (4in) apart from one another.

2 Fill the base of the bowl with a layer of pea gravel to an even depth of about 2.5cm (1in).

3 Next, add the compost, filling the bowl to just below the rim. Break up any large clumps of compost.

4 Select your lettuce seedlings, planting the red and green ones alternately in a circle. They should be about 10cm (4in) apart – this is not a critical measurement but they should not be planted too close to one another or overcrowding will check their growth.

5 Carefully arrange the slate pieces around the young plants, taking care not to damage the delicate leaves. The compost needs to be well covered; this will stop any weed growth and keep the compost moist and cool.

6 Water well all around each plant and keep well watered throughout the season as they grow.

Left: *The red-veined leaves of giant red mustard and finely cut mizuna leaves provide decorative and tasty additions to a mixed leaf salad.*

Rainbow radishes

Radishes are usually grown as a quick-maturing crop between slower-growing vegetables. Crisp and peppery with beautiful white flesh, they are best eaten young, when the flesh is tender and the white, pink, yellow, purple or red skins have not yet become tough. Radishes will grow easily in containers, but do make sure that they are shaded from hot sun. A dry compost and too much heat will cause the radishes to bolt, making them woody and inedible.

After sowing from seed, you will have to thin out the seedlings to encourage the radishes to form – they are swollen stems and need room to grow. A gap of one or two centimetres between plants is fine as long as you harvest the radishes when small. It takes only a month for radishes to mature, making them an ideal crop to interest young children.

In this case, the radish seeds have been planted in square plastic serving bowls, which are inexpensive and available in a good choice of vibrant colours. Before planting, simply pierce the base of each bowl a few times to make some drainage holes.

you will need

- plastic serving bowls about 30cm (12in) square and 18cm (7in) deep
- electric drill or craft knife
- pea gravel
- John Innes No. 3 or similar multipurpose compost
- radish seeds, French Breakfast

Left: Pull the radishes gently out of the compost as they mature, leaving others more space to grow. Wash, trim off the roots and leaves and serve immediately with a little flaked sea salt.

greencare

Do experiment with some of the many different varieties of radish available, by sowing a new variety every two weeks during the summer and autumn months.

1 Make a few holes in the base of each bowl. This is easily done with a drill or, if the plastic is not too rigid, by cutting with a craft knife. Add a 2.5cm (1in) layer of gravel to promote good drainage.

2 Fill the bowls almost to their rims with compost, breaking up any large lumps and then firming it down in the bowl with the palm of your hand so that it is not too loose.

3 Sprinkle the seed thinly on the surface of the compost. Then tuck the packet down between the soil and the side of the bowl so that you can identify the variety of radish when it is ready to pick.

4 Take a small amount of compost in your hands and gently rub them together over each bowl, allowing a fine layer to cover the seeds.

Right: *If the seeds are sown regularly, at intervals of two weeks or so, you will be able to harvest enough radishes to keep you supplied for many months of the year.*

5 Water the surface of the compost gently with a fine spray so as not to dislodge the seeds or wash them to one side of the bowl. Place the bowls away from full sun and keep the surface of the soil moist.

6 When the seedlings have reached a height of about 7.5cm (3in), thin them out, allowing a space of 1–2cm (up to 1in) between each radish.

Colourful chard

green*care*

Keep the plants well watered and watch out for snails hiding on the undersides of the leaves during the day. At night they will be feeding and are easier to spot by torchlight.

One of the prettiest leaf vegetables to grow, chard comes in many colours. The vibrant pink stems of ruby chard are almost luminous when the sun shines through them. Bright Lights, the variety used here, is a mixture of pink, red, yellow, orange and white stems; these are less vigorous than other types (which can grow to be enormous) but are suitable for container cultivation.

Swiss chard, sometimes also known as seakale beet, is the parent of all the coloured chards. It has glossy, dark green, rather puckered leaves and brilliant-white, broad-ribbed stems. The stems last a long

Right: *The dazzling colour of the chard stems is echoed in the leaf veins.*

Below: *The simplicity of this white fibre-clay planter shaped to fit on a windowsill is the perfect way of showing off the dazzling leaves of Bright Lights chard. Fibre clay is lighter than fired clay but more substantial than fibreglass.*

time and will even carry on producing substantial leaves through a mild winter. Just a few chard plants will be enough to feed a family. They have deep roots and won't be happy in a shallow planter.

Chard is tolerant of most soils, but you will get a better crop from a rich compost mixed with well-rotted manure. Luckily, the plant is relatively free of pests, although in a wet season slugs and snails will enjoy taking a bite out of the young leaves. You could spread a light-coloured mulch of crushed seashells over the surface of the compost after planting. This prevents too rapid evaporation, reducing the need for watering.

Chard leaves should be cooked separately from the stems because they have different densities. The leaves can be used like spinach or sautéed and combined with olive oil, chilli, garlic and perhaps a little tomato for a wonderful pasta sauce. Braised stems can be served with a cheese sauce. Steamed stems cut into sections, cooled and served as a salad with olive oil and lemon juice, is a simple summer favourite.

green*care*

You can sow chard seed in late spring for harvesting during summer and autumn, and again later in the season, producing a continuous supply of this versatile vegetable through the winter until the early summer of the next year. Either sow *in situ* or sow in modules and transplant to the final position when the seedlings are about 5cm (2in) tall. They should be spaced at least 10cm (4in) apart – more if you want sturdier and stronger plants.

Spinach in a supermarket basket

Right: *The ubiquitous supermarket basket makes an ideal planter as it holds a lot of compost.*

Below: *Pick young tender leaves for salad, but if you want to cook the spinach, allow the plants to grow bushier before harvesting.*

Real spinach, as opposed to spinach beet, which is a close relative of chard, is a tender and sweet-tasting leaf crop. You can grow it all through the year, although in the hottest and driest months it tends to run to seed. Don't grow spinach in hot sun – a lightly shaded position will produce a healthy crop. Watering is very important; spinach does best in a loam-based, moisture-retentive compost.

In this case, spinach plants have been planted in an old supermarket basket. This container is a perfect size for the purpose and the regular grid pattern of the wire creates a pleasing decorative effect.

The basket has been lined with a hanging-basket liner, which cleverly incorporates a perforated plastic film on the inside to prevent too much evaporation through the wire frame. Use a rich compost and add some well-rotted manure to the mix. A mulch of pea gravel spread over the surface of the compost around the base of the plants will help to retain moisture and keep the compost cool.

greencare

You can sow spinach direct into your container. Alternatively, sow a few seeds in a small pot of seed compost and transfer the clump of seedlings into their final growing position when they are 2–3cm (about 1in) high. Thin the clump, leaving one or two plants together (the thinnings make a sweet addition to a green salad).

Carrot and beetroot in jazzy tubs

you will need

gimlet (a screw-ended tool for boring holes)

dibber

plastic or rubber garden trugs 30cm (12in) high and 35cm (14in) diameter

peat-free multipurpose compost with added loam-based compost

beetroot and carrot seeds

fine sand

green*care*

Beetroot, with its sweet earthy flavour, is an undemanding crop that can tolerate most conditions, although it needs regular watering in dry spells. If seed is sown too early, the plant may bolt; you could try a variety called Bolthardy, which is bolt-resistant.

Carrots and beetroots are both well suited to container growing and their vibrant colours make a brilliant contrast when grown in colourful plastic or rubber tubtrugs.

Eaten straight after harvest, either raw or lightly steamed, home-grown carrots retain all the sweetness that is so often missing from shop-bought ones. You can sow the fast-maturing varieties every few weeks to ensure a supply throughout summer and autumn. Sow the first crop in early spring, first mixing the tiny seeds with a little fine sand to make sure they are sown more thinly. As they grow, the seedlings should be thinned to avoid crowding and to allow the remaining plants to grow bigger. Water well and often, applying a liquid seaweed feed every two weeks to improve the yield.

There are many varieties of beetroot available, some with exotic names. Bulls Blood is an old reliable type, while the stunning Chioggia is fuchsia pink with paler stripes and sweet tender flesh. There are cylindrical types, which are easy to slice, and beautiful golden globes, such as Burpees Golden, that look wonderful on the plate. Sow from spring to midsummer for a continuous supply.

The leaves and stalks of beetroot are also good to eat. Eat them young in salads or chop and cook the older ones as you might spinach or chard – sauté them in a pan with olive oil and some chopped chilli and garlic, and serve with fresh pasta.

Above left: *It's easy to see when beetroot are ready for cropping, and all parts of the plant are edible, so nothing is wasted.*

Right: *These colourful rubber containers will hold a good deal of compost, making them ideal for growing carrots and beetroots. Sow seed in the tubs where they are intended to grow as they will be too heavy to move later if you change your mind.*

1 Turn each tubtrug upside down and make a few drainage holes in the base with the gimlet.

2 Fill the tubtrug to the rim with the mixed compost. The compost will settle down somewhat when watered.

3 Use the dibber to make small holes in the compost 5cm (2in) apart. Sow a few beetroot seeds into each hole.

4 Mix the carrot seeds with a little fine sand and sprinkle them thinly onto the surface of the compost. Push the seed packets into the edge of the compost to identify the beetroot and carrots.

5 Water well, using a watering can fitted with a fine rose, and wait for the first seedlings to emerge.

6 When the beetroot seedlings emerge and develop their first true leaves, thin them again to give the plants more growing space. Leave the carrots to grow for a little longer before you start to thin them.

Left: *The combination of the bright pink and deep purple of the beetroot looks stunning against the pink container, especially when the evening sun shines through the stalks of the young plants.*

summer favourites

New potatoes, tomatoes, aubergines, courgettes, peppers and chillies all are ready to harvest in summer.

Don't compare your crop of peppers to those you find in shops. Their uniform shape and unblemished appearance reflect the unnatural conditions in which they are grown. Your organic, slightly small, possibly misshapen peppers are probably more 'natural' than any peppers you can buy. Peppers are adaptable plants and thrive in the most unusual containers as long as they have enough rich compost and plenty of moisture. Place peppers indoors on a sunny windowsill if the weather is unfriendly, but remember to keep them well watered and fed.

It is possible to grow a whole year's supply of fiery chillies from just a few plants. They can be eaten fresh or strung together and hung up to dry above the stove or in the sun for later use. As a long season from sowing to harvest is necessary to allow them to ripen fully, I recommend buying young plants of named varieties – these will have been started off by a professional grower early in the year in optimum conditions. Like peppers, chillies need heat and humidity, and benefit from a fine-mist water spray morning and evening. Bring them inside when the nights get cold.

Courgettes are also easy to grow. They need good rich compost and plenty of space. There are several varieties of courgette, from dark green to pale green striped; there are even golden courgettes (slightly less productive than other varieties) and curious round ones. Pick them young to encourage the plant to continue producing. The large golden flowers are a delicacy in Italian cooking, but pick them only after the tiny courgette is visible behind (which means that the flower has been pollinated). One option at the end of the season is to allow a couple of courgettes to remain longer on the plant and grow into marrows. These are not as sweet as young courgettes but can be very good when stuffed, and economical too – a single stuffed marrow will feed a whole family.

Potatoes in woven sacks

you will need

polypropylene potato-growing sack or similar

seed potatoes: Charlotte second earlies and Pink Fir Apple maincrop

good mixed compost combined with some well-rotted manure

egg boxes or tray

Is there any reason for growing your own when potatoes are so readily available and cheap? It's not that you can't buy organic potatoes, nor that you can't find the variety you want. It is for the pure pleasure of the experience – the satisfying process that begins with the early chitting of the seed potatoes and moves on to the planting in rich compost, the earthing up, the anticipation of the harvest. If you cook them within minutes of the harvest, you will be in no doubt about the value of the exercise. Shop-bought potatoes taste utterly different from those that are sweet, fresh, organic and home grown.

Not much space is required to grow a few potatoes since they are easy to cultivate in all sorts of containers. Builders' sand bags or plastic dustbins are commonly used. This project uses purpose-made woven polypropylene sacks; the loose style of weave provides good drainage. Potatoes are packed for transport in sacks made from a lighter version of the same material – you could ask your local greengrocer to save some for you.

Right: *Potatoes grow happily in big plastic woven sacks and produce huge numbers of leaves. These help to keep the compost weed free and moist, encouraging a bigger crop of potatoes.*

Potato varieties

Potatoes are from the same family as aubergines and tomatoes, as is obvious from the similarities between the plants' flowers. There are hundreds of varieties of potato to choose from, so consult a seed catalogue to see which tastes and textures appeal to you. A potato variety will often be described as 'floury' or 'waxy' – I think the waxy types are superior and more adaptable in the kitchen.

Potatoes are divided into three types: first earlies, second earlies and maincrops. First and second earlies are also called new potatoes; they are small and sweet and have thin skins that can be rubbed off. First earlies are planted in mid spring for cropping in early summer and midsummer. Second earlies are planted about a month later for cropping from mid to late summer. Both these types can be harvested when the plants flower. Leaving the plants in the soil a little longer means that you will harvest bigger potatoes.

Maincrops are planted up to a month later than second earlies. These are the big potatoes that store well and are eaten through the winter. They are harvested in autumn after the stems (known as haulm) have died down.

1 Lay the seed potatoes in the egg boxes or tray and place in a cool, light and frost-free place to encourage the tubers to chit, or sprout. They are ready when the sprouts are short and dark green or purple, which usually takes about four to six weeks. A shortage of light will result in weak, etiolated shoots, which will affect the growth of the potato plant. Chitting gives the potatoes a head start and helps to produce a larger harvest.

2 Roll down the sides of the sack so that you can easily reach the base. Add compost to a height of about 10–15cm (4–6in) above the base. Choose five or six seed potatoes and from each rub off all but two or three sprouts at one end. Place the potatoes, sprouted end up, on top of the compost.

3 Bury the seed potatoes 15cm (6in) deep under more compost and wait for the sprouts to grow and break through the earth. This could take a couple of weeks – or longer, if the weather is very cold.

4 As the plant grows and the leaves emerge, cover them again. This is called earthing up – it is partly a precaution against frost for early planted varieties and partly to encourage lots of tubers to form along the stems, giving a bigger crop. As the crop grows, continue earthing up, unrolling the sack as necessary. In dry periods make sure you give the plants plenty of water.

5 When the Charlottes begin to flower, you know it won't be long before you can harvest them.

6 Dig out a sample potato to see what size they have reached, and leave the rest a little longer if you want larger tubers. Either tip out the compost and potato crop from the sack or dig out a few as required. The Pink Fir Apples are a maincrop variety, which should be harvested when the foliage dies back.

chitting

Chitting means leaving seed potatoes in a cool, light place to encourage sprouting. Chitted potatoes produce a quicker, heavier crop – in effect, it means that the early part of the growing process is speeded up. Put the seed potatoes in egg boxes and place them in a porch or on a windowsill in a cool room. During the next few weeks, stout green or purple shoots will appear at the top of each potato. Only three or four of these are needed, so you can rub off the rest at the time of planting.

green*care*

Potatoes need regular watering to produce healthy tubers. Plant them in a rich soil, mixing some well-rotted manure into the planting compost.

Potato blight, which is a serious disease, can be largely avoided by growing the early varieties. If the leaves look burnt, to avoid damage to the tubers, cut off the top growth. The tubers can then be dug up normally.

To preserve optimum flavour, harvest your early potatoes minutes before you are ready to cook them.

Vine tomatoes in a blue trug

you will need

large plastic trug

gravel or crocks for drainage

three varieties of young tomato plants

mixture of organic peat-free multipurpose compost and a loam-based compost

fresh comfrey leaves (optional)

tray of tagetes (French marigolds)

Vine tomatoes, also known as cordon tomatoes, need a deep spacious container, especially if you grow more than one variety together. A rich, well-balanced compost is essential. To ensure a healthy crop, when the fruits mature give the plants a weekly liquid feed; an organic tomato or seaweed feed is ideal.

Pinch out the side shoots as they appear between the stem and the leaves. Allow about five sets of flowers, then pinch out the growing tip, known as the leader. This stops the tomato plant growing taller and producing more flowers, and ensures that all the plant's energy goes into ripening the fruit.

Tomatoes are easy to grow from seed, and make a great plant for novice gardeners to try. Start them off early in the year in small pots sited in a warm place to encourage growth, then transfer the seedlings into larger pots so that the young plants can become sturdy enough to grow outside when all risk of frost has passed. It is important to get them going early so that you have a long cropping season during the warmest weather.

The large blue plastic trug with rope handles used here is just the sort of container that's discarded every day in skips and town dumps. Trugs of this kind are common on building sites, so keep your eyes open – you never know where you might come across containers that have great potential for your garden.

Tomato varieties

Home-grown tomato plants seem to produce tomatoes that are much more delicious than those on offer in supermarkets – and the fruit has that wonderful just-picked smell. Another great advantage of growing your own is that it allows you to try out wonderful varieties that will never be available commercially. Reading the tomato section of a seed catalogue is a mouthwatering experience and it can be hard to narrow down the list of varieties that interest you.

The appearance of the mature fruit may be a factor in your choice. Tomato colours range from deep orange to vermilion to clear yellow. Some varieties have stripes or blushes. There is also a pretty pink variety as well as a number of curious black versions.

Even more fascinating is the choice of shapes, from the huge beefsteak to the tiny cherry tomato. The elegant plum tomato, commonly used in Italian sauces, is particularly rewarding to grow.

Right: Growing tagetes underneath tomatoes is a well-tried and effective form of companion planting. The pungent smell of tagetes repels aphids, so organic gardeners plant them all around the vegetable beds. The vibrant orange of the flower heads makes a striking partner for the tomato trusses above.

blight

The worst enemy of the tomato is blight, which is a nasty disease that the tomato shares with its close relative the potato.

Blight is particularly prevalent during damp, humid summers. Plants that have been infected look as if their leaves have been burnt, while the fruits have blackened areas and become inedible.

The best way to avoid blight is to grow your plants under cover. This may not always be possible, but growing tomatoes in a container, away from other blight-affected plants, will help. In order to prevent an attack, you can try spraying plants with a copper fungicide (Bordeaux mixture).

Right: *Planting vividly coloured tagetes at the base of the tomato plants makes an exotic display as well as protecting the tomatoes against an unwelcome aphid attack.*

1 Make a series of drainage holes in the base of the trug. Add a layer of gravel or crocks and fill the trug with the mixed compost.

2 Add the young tomato plants, spacing them evenly in the compost. Take care not to damage their roots when removing them from pots.

3 Leave the plant labels beside the plants so that you can identify your crop later on and compare its taste with other tomatoes.

4 Plant the tagetes all around the tomatoes. As the tomatoes grow tall, the tagetes will bush out and remain low, covering the compost. Cordon or vine tomatoes need staking. Use sturdy canes pushed into the compost beside the plant. Tie the stems to the canes regularly as they grow.

green*care*

As the tomato fruits begin to ripen, remove a few of the lower leaves to allow the sun to reach the fruits, which will encourage the ripening process.

Bush tomatoes in a wire basket

green*care*

Tomatoes need a good rich compost. Use a multipurpose potting compost and add some John Innes No. 3 or a good loam-based growing medium. This aids moisture retention, which is one of the most important requirements when growing any crop in a container of any kind.

The plants also need a good soaking of water every day during hot weather and will benefit from a special tomato feed once a week when the fruit has set.

Most importantly, they need sun; in a cool summer it will be difficult to get all your tomatoes to ripen, but the unripe green ones make the most wonderful chutney.

Tomatoes, although strictly fruit, are probably the most popular 'vegetables' to grow and, as is evident from any seed catalogue, there is an unbelievable variety to choose from.

Tomatoes come in three different types: the bush, the cordon (or vine) and the tumbler. The bush is probably the easiest to grow because it doesn't need pinching out or pruning. The cordon tomato, which produces the heaviest crop, will grow and grow until you pinch out the top shoot; it needs tying in to a sturdy stake and should have all the side shoots removed (see page 82). The tumbler is small, bushy and ideal for growing in pots, particularly in hanging baskets (see page 88).

Window boxes or troughs are good for the more compact varieties of tomato; larger pots or trugs are suitable for the vine types; and the bush tomato will thrive in a variety of containers, including, as shown here, an old wire basket. Wire containers must be lined to conserve moisture. In this case, the lining consists of a roll of pressed felt specially designed for hanging baskets; it has a perforated plastic film on the inside and can be cut to fit any container with an unusual shape.

Above left: *Plenty of plump tomatoes ripening on the vine makes one of the most magical sights of summer.*

Right: *The tomato has been planted in an old potato harvesting basket and has been underplanted with some bush basil plants. This is a small-leaved compact basil, often referred to as Greek basil, a perfect and traditional herb to accompany lovely ripe tomatoes.*

Tumbling toms in a hanging basket

Tumbling Tom is a small, prolific tomato plant that's ideal when you don't have much space. It will grow happily in any sort of container as long as it is planted in a rich compost and fed from the time when the fruits begin to mature. Two or three plants in a window box will give you a heavy crop of sweet cherry tomatoes all summer.

Cherry tomatoes are perhaps the easiest tomatoes to grow. Being compact bushes, they don't need any pinching out. For tomatoes to thrive outside, they need to be in a warm place – against a sunny wall, for example, where the stone or brick will retain warmth after the sun has disappeared at the end of the day.

If you grow this variety of tomatoes in a hanging basket, you must be vigilant about watering and feeding. It may help to add a small quantity of water-retaining granules to the loam-based compost to ensure that the compost stays moist. In hot weather, water twice a day. Purpose-made hanging baskets of all kinds are available at garden centres. The one used in this project is a vintage wire basket that is extremely decorative. Hang the basket from an old cast-iron bracket, if you can find one.

green*care*

Sow the seed from late winter until early spring in individual pots and cover with compost to exclude the light. If you keep the pots in a warm place, the seeds should germinate in a week. Choose the sturdiest seedling in each pot and discard the rest. Allow it to grow, only putting the young plant outside to harden off when the weather warms up. Bring the plants in at night until early summer, when you can plant them in their permanent growing positions without fear of frost.

Tomatoes like an even temperature, and cold nights make their leaves curl. In fact, the leaves of all outdoor-grown tomatoes can look a bit sorry for themselves as the season develops. Rain, wind and variations in temperature all take their toll. Luckily, the tomato fruits are usually unaffected. You will notice that the hotter the weather the sweeter the fruit.

Left: *Little cherry tomatoes are a real treat to eat straight from the plant.*

Right: *Even one small plant grown in a hanging basket or window box will provide you with a respectable crop of tomatoes during the summer.*

1 Line the hanging basket with the moss, creating a thick, even layer around the sides and base, and filling any gaps.

2 Rest the lined basket in the spare bucket. Put some compost in the base and add a small amount of water-retaining granules (follow the manufacturer's instructions).

3 Fill the basket to the top with compost and make a hole in the centre large enough to take the tomato plant.

4 Place the tomato plant in the hole and secure it by firming it in with your fingers. Water well.

comfrey liquid

Fruit-producing plants such as tomatoes need a high-potash feed, that is one containing potassium, to encourage the plant's development and stamina. Specially formulated organic feeds are available, but you may like to make your own comfrey liquid if you have access to comfrey plants (see page 16). Comfrey is rich in minerals, and particularly high in potash.

Fill a suitable container, such as a rubber bucket, as here, or an old enamel bucket, with freshly cut comfrey leaves – pack them in tightly, cover with water and weight them down with a large stone, or something similar. Cover the bucket and stand it in a shady out of the way place. The reason for this is that the smell is truly awful.

After three or so weeks, decant the liquid into plastic milk bottles. (This is a really good way to reuse plastic bottles.) Be careful to label them clearly.

When you come to use the liquid, first dilute it 1-to-5 in water. Once the flowers have set on your tomato plants, give them a good feed of this liquid every week.

Freshly cut comfrey leaves make a brilliant mulch around the base of tomato plants. You could even chop some up and mix into the planting compost.

Aubergine in a rubber tub

Aubergines have amazing purple black fruits with skin as shiny as a mirror. The downy stem and leaves are unlike any other plant, although they are related to the tomato family. The plants may appear to be soft all over but take care when handling because there are some rather sharp spines, especially on the calyx at the top of the ripening fruit.

Aubergines need a warm summer to thrive and, although varieties have been bred to suit a northerly climate, the plants do not appreciate great fluctuations in temperature. Cold nights are not helpful. If you

grow aubergines in a container, place it against a warm wall or similar outside space. The heat absorbed from the sun during the day will radiate at night, helping to create good aubergine-growing conditions. The tub used in this project is made from recycled tyres.

If the plant grows well, it may need staking to prevent wind damage, especially if it is bearing several heavy fruits. If the flowers don't set fruit – which sometimes happens – it is usually because the weather is too cold and there are too few pollinating insects. One way to alleviate this problem is to spread the pollen from flower to flower with a small paintbrush. You can tell if pollination has been successful because a tiny swelling, which will eventually become the fruit, appears in the centre of the flower.

greencare

Underplanting with tagetes, or French marigolds, helps to deter aphids and keeps the aubergine plants healthy. The tagete flowers will not discourage slugs, however.

I recommend buying in young plants – a nursery will have started them early in the year in large heated greenhouses. It is becoming much easier to buy healthy organic plants for very reasonable prices.

Above left: *Exquisite lilac flowers, which are particularly inviting to bees, precede the distinctive, deep purple fruit.*

Right: *You can't help feeling proud when your aubergine plant produces a beautiful dark shiny fruit. The rubber tub makes a deep and roomy container for this lovely vegetable.*

Right: *A bright green can, which once contained olives, makes a useful and unusual container for this beautiful aubergine plant. I didn't even have to cut away the top since it had a large circular lid that, when removed, left a perfect planting hole. Although they appear to be soft all over, take care when handling aubergine plants because there are some rather sharp spines, especially on the calyx at the top of the ripening fruit.*

1 Cut some drainage holes in the tub base. It is simplest to cut a triangle with each side 1cm (½in) long. Fill the tub with the mixed compost to within 2cm (1in) of the rim.

2 Make a hole in the centre. Remove the aubergine plant from its pot and place in the hole. Firm the compost gently around the plant.

3 Plant the tagetes equidistantly around the aubergine. To make the tagetes bushier, pinch out the central growing tip – this will encourage the plant to produce more sideshoots with more potential for flowers. As the aubergine grows, add a stake and tie the stem to it with garden twine at regular intervals.

Right: *The skin of a ripe aubergine is tight and shiny – like a curved mirror, it reflects the dazzling orange flowers of the companion tagetes.*

Chillies in olive-oil cans

you will need

olive-oil can

can opener

hammer

thick long nail

terracotta crocks or gravel

multipurpose compost mixed with loam-based compost

young chilli plant

Chillies can be really prolific plants and it is quite possible to grow enough to last you all year. You can use some of the fresh chillies as they ripen and then dry the remainder for storage and use throughout the winter – simply lay them out on a tray covered with a clean cloth and leave in a warm place to dessicate slowly. Alternatively, thread them together in bunches on a long piece of string and hang them in a warm, dry place.

Chillies will thrive in warm weather outside but they generally prefer quite humid conditions. When growing chillies inside on a sunny windowsill, keep them damp by watering with a fine spray. If the plants or soil dry out, they are liable to drop their buds.

These colourful and exotic plants deserve to be grown in equally decorative containers. Empty olive-oil cans printed with interesting text and images are ideal. You can ask your local restaurant or health-food store to save them for you – in this way, you could build up quite a collection, enough to contain a whole family of assorted chilli plants. These metal planters will last for a few years outside before rust penetrates and they begin to fall apart.

Right and below: *Chillies grow quite happily in containers. A number of different cans with a few varieties of chilli makes a decorative display – and these plants are a useful crop to grow. Dry your chillies at the end of the season when they are ripe and you will have enough to last until the next growing season.*

green*care*

The seeds germinate rapidly and can be sown in early spring inside. Sow in small pots and prick out the seedlings, leaving the strongest one in each pot. When the weather warms up, transfer the young plant into your chosen container. Use a rich compost and, as the small chillies start to form, feed with a high-potash liquid feed.

If you don't have time to grow chillies from seed, it is easy to find named varieties in a good plant nursery. They will be raised and sold alongside their close relatives, peppers, tomatoes and aubergines.

Only you will know how hot you like your chillies – some are sweet and only slightly fiery, while others are unbearably hot. Seed catalogues indicate the intensity of different varieties, and young commercially grown plants will often be labelled with the level of heat.

I recommend growing a variety of types of chilli, from mild to hot, and a variety of shapes and colours, from red, green and yellow to the more unusual black.

1 Remove the top of the can using a can opener. Smooth any sharp burrs on the metal rim by banging a hammer around the rim. Make four holes in the base with the nail.

2 Turn the can the right way up and put a 5cm (2in) layer of broken crocks or gravel in the base. This will encourage good drainage.

3 Fill the can to the rim with the mixed compost. Shake it down and then add some more. Break up any large lumps of compost.

4 Make a hollow in the compost. Tap the chilli plant out of its pot and plant in the can. Firm in the plant with your hands. Water well.

greencare

As the plant grows, you may need to use a small stake to support it because the chillies can become quite heavy. If you keep picking the chillies, the plant will continue to produce more. To prolong the harvest, bring the plant inside at the end of the summer.

Right: *These fiery red chillies have been planted in a small galvanized bucket. They are ripe when the skin begins to wrinkle slightly; pick and use immediately, or dry and store for future use.*

Red and yellow peppers in a plastic basket

I love the intense colours and intricate patterns of woven plastic baskets. They are also very light and extremely durable – both desirable qualities in a planter – and many have handles, making them easy to move around.

This basket is lined with a green refuse sack; the top of the sack is rolled down and hidden behind the rim of the basket after the compost

has been added. Don't forget to cut a few slits in the base of the sack and add a few crocks of broken polystyrene to promote good drainage.

It is advisable to buy in peppers as young plants. To raise them from seed, you need to sow very early in order for the plants to be advanced enough to grow and ripen during the summer. The hotter the temperature the quicker the peppers will mature, of course. In a cool summer, you could grow this plant on a sunny windowsill to make the most of the heat of the sun.

Peppers come in many shapes, colours and sizes. Don't be surprised if yours don't look like the ones you can buy. Shop-bought peppers are always grown in controlled conditions with little fluctuation in temperature, and any misshapen fruit will be discarded rather than being put on sale.

green*care*

As with most container-grown produce, peppers should be watered often and, especially during hot weather, in the evening. This deters the roots from rising to find the water and getting scorched near the heated surface of the compost. Give a weekly liquid feed once the fruit has matured.

Above left: *Pick the fruit as the colour deepens, as this will encourage more peppers to form*

Right: *A couple of pepper plants will thrive in this colourful woven bicycle basket. They need a warm summer and moist conditions.*

Courgettes in a galvanized bath

you will need

old galvanized metal bath

hammer and large nail

bucket of gravel (for drainage)

peat-free compost

John Innes No. 3

well-rotted horse manure

bucket of comfrey leaves (if available)

blood, fish and bone fertilizer

two or three courgette plants

Vintage galvanized domestic and agricultural items, such as baths, buckets, trays, watering cans and grain bins, are becoming sought after as practical planters. There is something about the gentle grey of the metal and the pleasing shapes and proportions of these objects that makes them ideal containers for plants. They are lightweight and good at retaining moisture – none evaporates through the non-porous sides.

Courgettes are large, thirsty, hungry plants that need a large container – a bath is an ideal size. They are easy to grow and, given the right conditions, they romp away, creating a virtual jungle of stems and leaves. Courgettes become slightly bitter if they are not eaten immediately after harvest. Pick them often – if they are allowed to grow too large, the plant will be less productive.

If you don't have enough space to start them inside, you can sow courgettes direct into their permanent position, but wait until late spring. You could make a mini cloche from a plastic water bottle for added protection. Alternatively, buy young plants from a garden centre or nursery or plant sale; many varieties are available and, since you will need only two or three plants, this is a sensible option.

Above: *The beautiful golden flowers of the courgette are edible and delicious. Pick them after the courgette has formed. The flowers are usually dipped in a light batter and fried in olive oil. In Italy they are a delicacy and are often served stuffed with anchovy or mozzarella cheese.*

Right: *Although a plant carries both male and female flowers, the courgette fruit forms behind female flowers only.*

Courgette varieties
There are many varieties of courgette, ranging in colour and shape from golden yellow (a less vigorous plant) to dark shiny green, striped or pale-skinned, and from long to globe-shaped. Grow two or three varieties and see which you like. Start them off in spring under cover or inside. Push the flat seeds down into a seed compost in individual pots – you can sow two seeds together and remove the weaker seedling as they grow.

1 With the bath the right way up and resting on soft ground, make a number of drainage holes evenly in the base with the hammer and nail.

2 Empty the bucket of gravel into the bath and spread evenly across the base. This layer will encourage good drainage.

3 Mix together the two composts in equal quantities and empty into the bath, covering the gravel to a depth of about 10cm (4in).

4 Collect the comfrey leaves and chop them roughly. Cover the compost with a thick layer of chopped leaves. This will provide a rich nutritional boost to the growing plants as the roots reach down.

green*care*

If you can't find fresh comfrey leaves to mix in with the compost, you could feed the courgettes weekly with a diluted tomato or seaweed extract instead.

5 Fill up the bath to the rim with the mixed composts, this time adding one part well-rotted manure to four parts compost.

6 Sprinkle the blood, fish and bone fertilizer on the surface of the compost. (First read the manufacturer's instructions and don't use too much.) Lightly dig it in.

7 Plant the young courgettes equidistantly and firm down the soil around them. Water well. Keep the compost moist and never let the soil dry out.

Right: *Courgettes love warm weather and will soon produce a canopy of large leaves on sturdy hollow stems. The leaves shelter the growing vegetables from the direct heat of the sun and reduce evaporation of moisture from the soil.*

Nasturtiums in a metal bucket

Right: The rich vermilion of the bush variety of nasturtiums contrasts well with the chalky-blue painted galvanized mop bucket.

Below: Use the open young flowers and small leaves as a colourful and peppery addition to a fresh summer salad.

The vibrantly coloured flowers and strange circular leaves of nasturtiums are edible as well as good-looking. They have a peppery, mustard-like flavour and make a brilliant addition to summer salads. There are many kinds of nasturtium, from compact bushy plants to trailing or climbing versions, and they come in a rich variety of warm colours, from brilliant orange to rich mahogany. Sow the large seeds once and you will have them forever, since they are prodigious self-sowers. They germinate quickly and can be sown until midsummer. Nasturtiums do best in poor soil; too much goodness encourages leaves at the expense of flowers.

Later in the season, you could grow a climbing nasturtium as a partner to a squash or a decorative gourd, allowing it to scramble up and over an arch, obelisk or loose structure of canes or sticks. Don't plant too many nasturtiums, though, or their vigorous habit will overwhelm everything else.

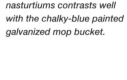

green*care*

Nasturtiums are often grown as companion plants to tomatoes because their pungent smell repels whitefly. They can also be grown as a sacrificial plant around broad beans; the pest blackfly, which can attack the tips of beans, much prefers the buds and leaves of nasturtiums.

bean feast

Beans of all kinds are easy to grow. They suffer from few pests or diseases and tolerate most weather conditions. They are highly nutritious – either eat the young green pods or leave some varieties on the plant to ripen into beans to be dried for eating in winter.

Dwarf beans produce a smaller crop than their climbing relations. Sow at least twice during the summer to extend the cropping time or pick the beans small and young. A plant must produce seed to propagate itself the following year, and regular picking encourages it to produce more.

Climbing beans ripen from the base upwards and crop for a few weeks from midsummer. Runner beans, in particular, with crimson flowers held high above the leaves as an invitation to bees, have often been grown for decorative purposes. Curiously, climbing French beans are pollinated by the wind and do not need insects.

Beans for drying, such as crimson-speckled borlotti, can be left on the withering vine to ripen in late summer sun. Thoroughly dry them before storage to inhibit any mould growth. To encourage drying, lay them on a tray indoors in a warm place for a few days.

Broad beans are hardy, so plant in autumn or early winter for harvesting in early summer the following year. They are quick to germinate – it is one of the most exciting things for a gardener to see the new stem of the bean pushing through the compost. You can plant directly in the soil when this has warmed slightly after the winter, or plant in biodegradable pots that can be transferred into the soil.

Peas are a little more difficult to grow, but worth the effort. Peas need a rich soil and should be well watered, but do not allow them to become over-wet. They also dislike hot dry sun. You may need to throw a net loosely over the crop to protect it from birds.

Known collectively as legumes, beans and peas 'fix' nitrogen in the soil by producing small nodules on the roots. At the end of the season, dig the roots into the compost and the nodules will feed the soil. This also works in containers – it's a natural plant feed.

Dwarf French beans in a round basket

you will need

round cylindrical basket
paper potter
newspaper
heavy-duty plastic garden refuse sack
seed tray
dwarf French beans
multipurpose compost mixed 3:1 with well-rotted manure
seed compost

French beans will grow happily in a container as long as the soil is rich and moist. They are prolific croppers and will provide a good harvest over four to six weeks. You can extend the cropping time by sowing more beans four weeks after the first batch; this is known as successional sowing (you will need another container in which to plant this later crop). As the second sowing will take place later in the year, when the air temperature is warmer, the beans can be sown directly into the container. The earlier crop should be sown individually in long pots. When the plants start to flower, feed them weekly with a liquid manure or seaweed extract to ensure a long-lasting crop.

The deep, round basket used here is an ideal size in which to grow five dwarf French beans. It is lined with a garden-refuse sack, which stops water leaking from the basket – but don't forget to make some drainage holes in the base. Another advantage of using a basket is that it is lightweight – if you are growing crops on a roof terrace, you need to be careful about how much weight you are introducing.

Above: *Pick your beans just before you cook them for the best flavour.*

Right: *Don't be tempted to include too many plants in your container. Five make a really bushy group and will produce a good crop of lovely crisp stringless green beans.*

1 Make some newspaper pots using the paper potter (see page 24). Fill each pot with sowing compost. Make a hole in the centre of the compost with a stick and push one bean into each hole. Cover the bean with compost.

2 Water the beans and put the pots in a plastic coldframe or bring inside and place on a cool windowsill to allow the beans to germinate.

3 Push the plastic sack well into the basket and roll the edge around the top rim. Make a few slits in the bottom for drainage.

greencare

Beans go well with summer savory, which resembles thyme. Coincidentally, summer savory can also be grown as a companion plant to beans, warding off aphids with its powerful aroma.

4 Place a few sheets of folded newspaper in the base to aid moisture retention. Add the well-mixed compost and manure and fill the basket to the brim.

5 Remove the plastic sack from the rim of the basket, roll up and tuck inside beneath the compost.

Right: *When the flowers appear and the small beans start to form, you may need to give the plants some support. Tying them with string to a few bamboo canes will stop them flopping over the edge of the basket.*

6 Plant the young beans in the basket, still inside their paper pots, when the first two real leaves have emerged. Space them widely – about five will be plenty in this size of basket.

7 Soak the beans with water poured from a watering can fitted with a fine rose, and place in a warm, protected, sunny position.

Petit pois in galvanized buckets

you will need

biodegradable containers, such as paper pots (see page 24)

galvanized bucket

hammer

long nail

gaffer tape

peat-free compost

well-rotted manure

old newspaper

comfrey leaves (if available)

bundle of pea sticks

Right: *Pick peas before they swell to fill the pod too tightly or they will taste rather starchy.*

If you buy peas, it really is only worth buying them frozen – freezing immediately after harvest preserves the natural sugars in the pea, which otherwise quickly turn to starch, destroying the fresh sweet taste. For the same reason, home-grown peas eaten soon after harvest taste far better than so-called fresh peas in the pod bought in a supermarket.

A fairly deep container is needed to grow peas, and you must be careful to water the plants very regularly. Since peas are climbers, they will also need a structure to grow up. Peas love a rich moist soil. If you put newspaper at the base of the container, it will help to preserve moisture, and a layer of the magical comfrey plant will add a wealth of nutrients, promoting healthy growth as the leaves rot down in the soil. Peas are leguminous plants that add nitrogen to the soil through small nodules on their deep roots. At the end of the season, cut down the plants and leave the roots intact; the soil will still be fertile and can be planted with a late-cropping salad.

Pea sticks are traditionally used when peas are grown in a row in a vegetable garden. They are attractive and can be made from a variety of woody stems. These are usually cut in winter from hazel, but beech, lime, hornbeam and birch are also excellent. Choose a twiggy branch.

1 Plant two or three pea seeds early in the year in a biodegradable pot. Keep them well watered and frost free, allowing the shoots to grow strongly.

2 Turn the galvanized bucket upside down and stick four short pieces of gaffer tape on to the base, spacing them evenly. Place the nail on each strip of tape in turn and bang firmly with the hammer to make a hole.

3 Turn the bucket right way up. Place some newspaper in the bottom of it and cover with a handful of freshly cut comfrey leaves.

4 Tip in the well-mixed compost and manure until the bucket is almost full to the brim (the level will settle and drop after watering).

5 Plant the individual pots of peas into the compost. Five pots is about right for this size of container. Firm them in with your hands and, when all are planted, water thoroughly.

green*care*

Peas can dry out rapidly in containers and they particularly dislike being baked by the sun. Keep them moist by watering in the morning, but do not overwater. As the first peas start to develop, a weekly liquid feed of seaweed is essential. When the peas start to ripen, pick regularly; this will encourage them to continue producing.

6 Finally, push the pea sticks into place around the peas. Try to make the twigs all face inwards. You can weave them together slightly to achieve this.

petit pois and sweet peas

Sweet peas with their charming frilly, fragrant flowers are traditionally grown alongside vegetables. They can even be grown in the same container as petit pois because they like the same conditions. Fortunately, since they make a lovely cut-flower display, sweet peas need to be picked and deadheaded on a regular basis to prolong their flowering season. There is no danger of mistaking the hairy coarse pods of the sweet pea for the much more appetizing edible variety.

Above: *Sweet peas and edible peas make lovely companions; some varieties of edible pea also have colourful flowers, particularly the purple flowering mange tout.*

Right: *The twining tendrils of the pea vine search out and quickly attach themselves to the twiggy branches of the pea sticks.*

Broad beans in a coconut sack

Broad beans are a treat. Easy to grow, they are one of the earliest vegetables to crop and they taste delicious. Seed is traditionally planted in early winter for cropping in early summer. This won't work well in containers since the relatively small volume of soil may mean that the beans freeze during a cold winter, so plant the seeds in early spring in seed compost contained in cardboard tubes, such as those in the middle of lavatory rolls or kitchen rolls. Stand the tubes in a tray and keep them under a cloche until the weather gets warmer.

You can also grow the bean seedlings inside on a cool windowsill. The large seeds germinate quickly if the temperature is not too low. When the young plants are 10cm (4in) high, they can be planted out in their permanent position, still in the cardboard tubes. The roots will happily penetrate the cardboard tubes, which will quickly biodegrade in the moist soil.

Many vegetables are transported in the type of synthetic woven sack used here as a planting container – you could ask your local greengrocer to save some for you. There is no need to put any drainage crocks at the base of the sack because the close weave will allow moisture to escape freely. During hot weather, water the plants every day and take great care never to let the compost dry out.

Right: A synthetic vegetable sack, often used for packing and transporting potatoes and root crops, makes an unusual and practical planter.

Below: The highly scented black-and-white flowers, which bloom all the way up the stem, are adored by bees; young beans are forming at the base while the tops are still producing flowers.

greencare

The worst pest as far as broad beans are concerned is blackfly, but this can be warded off by pinching out the growing tips at the top of the stems. This will also encourage the pods to form.

Beans are hungry feeders and like rich soil, so incorporate some well-rotted manure into the multipurpose compost in a proportion of 3:1 compost to manure. The manure will also help the compost to retain water.

Borlotti beans in laundry baskets

Perhaps the most decorative vegetables, climbing beans have twining stems studded with flowers of many colours. Runner beans, with their abundant scarlet flowers held on upright stems above lush green leaves, have long been valued for their appearance as well as their taste. Many more types are now available, with flowers ranging from white to pink, apricot and orange. Why not grow a mixture of beans together up a bamboo 'wigwam'? Look in seed catalogues or garden centres and nurseries for varieties that can be sown at the same time.

The delicious and nutritious borlotti bean, a key ingredient of minestrone soup and other Italian dishes, has fat, cream-coloured pods speckled with red blotches. Although not such a heavy cropper as other beans, its particular qualities mean that no vegetable garden should be without it. Unlike French and runner beans, borlotti beans are harvested from the pods before cooking. They are best eaten fresh, although they can be dried for winter use.

The sturdy cylindrical laundry basket used here is ideal. It has been painted with a shed or fence paint, which will help to prolong its life. Lining the basket with a strong plastic bag, in this case an empty compost bag, is essential to retain moisture. An added advantage, especially if you are growing vegetables on a balcony, is that the basket is much lighter than a conventional pot of a similar size.

Left: *As the beans ripen in late summer, the pods, originally cream speckled with red, turn a fiery crimson. Pick, remove the nutritious beans from the pods and use fresh.*

Right: *The sturdy bean plants twine tightly round the support rods or canes – they grow quickly at this stage.*

green*care*

To grow borlotti beans, you will need a fairly deep rich soil that has some well-rotted manure incorporated into the compost. Planting the beans in a deep container allows a lengthy root run and means that the compost will retain moisture. Keep the plants well watered, remembering to water in the evening on hot days. Like other leguminous (pea-like) plants, borlotti beans are thirsty and hungry feeders. They will tolerate some shade but need the warmth of the summer to ripen the pods.

1 Paint the basket following the instructions on the can. You may need to apply two coats to achieve complete coverage. Paint to a depth of 10cm (4in) inside the rim. Allow to dry thoroughly.

2 Insert the compost sack, having first cut a few slits in the base to allow for drainage. Roll the top edge over so that it fits snugly inside the basket rim.

3 Mix the compost and the manure at a ratio of roughly 3:1. Throw a few crocks or stones into the base of the basket to help with drainage before adding the compost. Fill the last 20cm (8in) with multipurpose compost.

4 Make some holes with a dibber about 10cm (4in) apart and sow one or two beans in each hole. You can remove the weaker of the two beans later.

5 Water the basket well, but make sure the water does not expose the planted beans.

6 Cover the beans with glass to raise the temperature of the soil. This will encourage the beans to sprout.

7 When the first true leaves have appeared, push a rod or cane into the earth beside it – the beans will quickly twine around it.

green*care*

If you grow runner or climbing French beans, pick them regularly to ensure a continuing crop. Allow borlotti beans to swell in the pod before harvesting. If you want to dry them, allow the pods to shrivel slightly on the vine before picking for storage.

fruits and berries

Even if you have only a small outdoor space, you can still grow some of your own fruit. Many fruit-bearing plants grow happily in containers and some orchard trees have been bred especially for this purpose.

Grape vines thrive if grown in a warm, sunny place. They need a large container with enough soil to retain moisture, and should be pruned regularly to reduce leafy growth and promote a well-formed plant that will yield a fair harvest. As well as being productive, grape vines look wonderful when the leaves take on vibrant colours in autumn. A good nursery will advise on the best type of vine for your climate and conditions. In my opinion, the muscat-flavoured grapes are the best.

Strawberries are perhaps the easiest of all fruit to grow in containers. Both cultivated strawberries and the wild or alpine type need to be kept moist and will tolerate some shade. Wild strawberries are a real treat and always a favourite with children. Allow the berries to ripen fully to a dark red colour and then pick them to eat straight from the plant.

Many currants and berries – redcurrants, whitecurrants, blackcurrants, gooseberries and blueberries – are easy to grow in containers and produce masses of fruit. Originating in north America, blueberries are increasingly popular in Europe. New varieties have been bred to suit European conditions, and you can now buy blueberry plants that fruit in early, middle or late season.

Physalis, or cape gooseberries, are easy to grow and generally not attacked by pests or diseases. Seeds germinate quickly, or you can buy young plants. Like tomatoes, to which they are closely related, physalis need warmth and sun to ripen (berries will ripen indoors if left on a windowsill).

All fruit will benefit from a weekly high-potash liquid feed when the fruit begins to mature. A tomato feed is ideal; organic varieties are readily available.

Blueberries in a dolly tub

Above: *The small, attractive berries ripen from pale green to deep purple.*

Right: *Blackbirds love ripe blueberries. You can ward them off by loosely draping a piece of garden netting over the whole bush as the berries begin to turn blue.*

green*care*

Blueberries must be grown in ericaceous (slightly acid) compost, which is available, specially formulated, from garden centres. The soil should be kept moist, so it is best to stand the pot in a semi-shaded position. If you can use rain water for watering, it will help to maintain the acid conditions of the soil.

Blueberries, one of the sweetest fruits, are fairly easy to grow in pots. They look particularly good planted in any galvanized container, but they need plenty of space to thrive. A dolly tub (an old washtub) is ideal. Most tubs of this kind have a ribbed design and a decorative rim. They have become rather fashionable and collectable and can be found in vintage shops and markets, as well as at farm sales.

The blueberry plant grows into an attractive medium-sized bush with bell-shaped, pale ivory flowers in late spring and beautiful autumn foliage. The berries, which grow in clusters, gradually ripen over a few weeks, turning from pale sage green to dark blue fruits covered in a bloom.

A fully mature bush will provide you with a daily handful of nutritious berries for a few weeks during the summer. If you have space, you can prolong the harvesting time by growing an early, a mid-season and a late-cropping variety. Before buying a young plant from a nursery, note what the label says about cropping time – it would be a shame to buy a variety that crops in midsummer while you are away on holiday.

Strawberries in wooden fruit boxes

you will need

old wooden fruit or wine boxes

plastic woven potato sack for lining

sharp sand

compost

well-rotted horse manure

large staple gun

Strawberries are very well suited to being cultivated in containers, but to achieve a successful crop you need to follow a few basic rules. Choose a humus-rich, moisture-retaining compost and mix in bonemeal and well-rotted manure before planting. To cut down on water loss, line your container with woven plastic sack fabric. Strawberries, particularly the delicious alpine variety, can tolerate a little shade.

Regular feeding with a seaweed extract will ensure large and healthy fruits. Straw placed around the ripening plants will keep them clean, and its light colour will raise the temperature around the fruit by reflecting the light. You may have to net the fruits as they ripen to protect them from birds.

1 Cut the potato sack into two pieces. Place one piece inside the box, folding over the edges before stapling in place. Use the other piece to cover the rest of the wood.

2 Put a layer of sharp sand over the base to improve drainage.

Above left: *Once the flowers appear, make sure the box is near other flowering plants to encourage bees to visit.*

Right: *An old wooden fruit box stamped on the slatted sides with the name of the grower makes an attractive and practical container in which to grow strawberries.*

green*care*

Some gardeners put the strawberries into a glass jar when they are green, creating a mini greenhouse to speed up ripening. This also has the advantage of protecting them from birds.

3 Add a generous layer of compost to the box, covering the sandy base.

4 Add a layer of manure and mix well. Mix in more compost and some bonemeal.

5 Plant the strawberry plants equidistantly from one another in the box, pressing down the compost firmly around them.

6 The plants will grow quickly. If you keep them well watered, they will produce many flowers. Watch out for pollinating insects at this point. When the strawberries begin to set, place some clean straw underneath and around them, to lift them off the compost.

potting up strawberry runners

Strawberries are very obliging plants. After flowering, they start to send out long stems, known as runners, from the crown of the parent plant. If potted up, a runner produces roots and becomes a new healthy plant ready to produce fruit for the next season.

Above: *The six plants cultivated in this wooden box could produce at least twenty new plantlets.*

Right: *Fill a pot with loam-based compost. Place a plantlet in the centre of the pot and 'pin' it in place with a hairpin-shaped piece of strong garden wire. Leave this plantlet attached to the parent plant until fully rooted, at which point it can be detached. Plant out in the autumn in a new container.*

Alpine strawberries

Plant up alpine strawberries in the same way as that described for dessert strawberries on pages 128–131. They will ripen earlier and go on fruiting for longer than their larger counterparts. The tiny pointed fruits are produced on high stems, often above the leaves. Curiously, birds don't seem particularly interested in the alpine variety.

Right and far right: *Alpine strawberries are easy to grow, delicious and luckily they go on producing fruit for the whole summer. They are happy to grow in part shade as they originate in clearings and on the edges of alpine forests.*

A bowl of physalis

Physalis is beautiful bushy plant related to the potato family and, like the potato, it originated in South America. It is widely cultivated around the world, and grown commercially in South Africa – hence its common name of Cape gooseberry. Related varieties may be known as strawberry tomato or ground cherry.

The flowers are exquisite and unusual, hanging timidly down from the leaf axils. As they grow, they develop into delicate papery lanterns

which enclose the deep yellow berries. When ripe, they have a delicious musky taste and are used as a garnish on cakes and in fruit salads; they make a wonderful jam if you can harvest enough of them.

Physalis is a vigorous, easy-to-grow plant that will happily self-seed in the right conditions, but it dislikes a soil that is too rich. Although it can be sown from seed early in the year, you may find it easier or more convenient to buy ready-grown young plants at the right time to plant outside. You will find them for sale alongside young tomato plants in early summer. The fruits ripen late in the summer – to see if they are sweet and ready to eat, pick one and try it. They will ripen from the base of the plant upwards (rather like tomatoes) and will continue to crop over a few weeks.

Above left: *The pale yellow flowers with chocolate spot centres are unique and intriguing. They appear evenly all over the plant where the leaves attach to the stem.*

Above right: *Each fruit is enclosed by a papery lantern that begins a pale green and gradually turns to a straw yellow as the enticing yellow fruit within ripens.*

Right: *Physalis grows well in containers. Its fruit makes an unusual and refreshing addition to salads and desserts, and can also be made into jams and jellies.*

greencare

Since physalis plants are easy to grow, they will adapt to a variety of containers as long as the pots are deep enough to contain the roots and hold sufficient water. As well as being a pretty shape and colour, this enamel washing bowl is ideal – any metal container, being non-porous, has the advantage of conserving moisture in the soil. Punch a few holes in the base of the bowl and add a layer of gravel or clay pot crocks to promote good drainage. Finish with a hard mulch of stones, china shards or shells to prevent unnecessary moisture loss from the surface of the compost.

Pot-grown grape vine

Perhaps surprisingly for such vigorous plants, grape vines will thrive in large containers. To produce worthwhile fruit, they need warmth and sun. A south- or southwest-facing wall is ideal, providing shelter and radiated heat from daytime sunshine. Grape vines are decorative climbing plants with deeply cut leaves that provide a mellow autumnal

show as the bunches of black or white grapes ripen in late summer. Look for an outdoor type that suits your location. Good garden centres will offer a small variety of vines, but for more specialist advice consult a dedicated grower.

Grape vines need a rich loam-based compost. When the grapes have matured, feed the plant weekly with a high-potash feed – liquid comfrey or tomato food is fine. Regular pruning and training is essential. In early summer, prune the young green shoots, known as laterals, to two leaves beyond the flowers or young grapes. In winter, prune back severely to the wood, a short distance beyond the previous year's growth. It's worth consulting a book or magazine with step-by-step instructions for pruning – when you've done it once, you'll know what to do each year.

You will be able to grow enough grapes to have a good few bunches to eat as fruit. Alternatively, you could make a small quantity of wine, grape juice or jelly. Even the leaves are edible (after being pickled in brine), being widely used in Greek cooking to make little parcels stuffed with rice and minced meat.

greencare

A grape vine needs a large container – one that can hold enough compost to feed the roots and to make a firm anchor to stop the plant becoming top heavy and pulling the pot over. The clay pot used here is a simple version of the traditional terracotta pot in which grape vines are so often grown.

If you want to train a grape vine up an obelisk or grow it on a frame of canes, you need to tie in the laterals repeatedly until you have the size and shape of vine that you want.

Above left: *Given the right conditions, grapes will thrive in containers.*

Right: *This grey clay planter attractively complements the ripe black grapes it contains. A vine is happiest sited in the sunniest position in the garden. Mulch the surface of the compost with an assortment of decorative pebbles.*

Red and whitecurrants

Right: *The glistening berries of the redcurrant are the jewels of the fruit garden. One bush can produce enough berries to make a few pots of delicious jam or jelly.*

Far right: *Whitecurrants are heavy croppers and curiously they are sweeter to taste than the ruby red berries of the redcurrant. The berries can be picked in one go when they are all fully ripe. Test for ripeness by tasting.*

green*care*

All currants can grow well in large containers, but they need to be kept moist and should not be in relentless full sun. Since currant bushes are perennials, you will need to refresh, feed and replenish the compost each spring.

Currants come in three types: blackcurrants, redcurrants and whitecurrants. These tender berries really are worth growing yourself, since it is unusual to find them in the shops – they are laborious to pick and don't travel well. Blackcurrants, the largest of the three, are a deep purple black; they are tart and best eaten cooked, making excellent jam, pies and puddings. The smaller redcurrants with their glistening vermilion berries grow in delicate bunches called strings. They are much sought after by garden birds and need to be netted. The similar but sweeter whitecurrants generally escape the ravages of the birds, which are not attracted by their pale translucent berries.

Redcurrants and whitecurrants are delicious eaten fresh. Both varieties also make lovely clear jellies – add some chopped home-grown red chilli to make an excellent accompaniment to meat and poultry dishes.

Useful addresses

Allotment Growing
www.allotment.org.uk
Personal site with a great deal of
advice on all aspects of allotment
gardening and vegetable growing,
as well as a forum and recipes to
use for your produce.

BBC Gardening
www.bbc.co.uk/gardening
Advice on all aspects of gardening,
including growing crops in pots.

Garden Organic
(previously HDRA)
Garden Organic Ryton
Coventry
Warwickshire CV8 3LG
Tel: 02476 303517
www.gardenorganic.org.uk
Offers advice and information
about courses on organic
gardening.

Green Gardener
Brook Hill
Brundall Road
Blofield NR13 4LB
Tel: 01603 715096
www.greengardener.co.uk
Specialists in safe, effective
biological pest controls, which are
harmless to children, pets and
wildlife.

Just Green Ltd
Unit 14
Springfield Road Industrial Estate
Burnham-on-Crouch
Essex CM0 8UA
Tel: 01621 785088
sales@just-green.com
Natural pest control and gardening
products, as well as other
household products.

Let's Go Gardening
www.letsgogardening.co.uk
General gardening information.

Rocket Gardens
Wheal Sara Farm
Horsedowns
Camborne
Cornwall TR14 ONP
01209 831468
www.rocketgardens.co.uk
Mail-order online company which
organically grows and distributes
vegetable and herb seedlings
throughout the UK

Royal Horticultural Society
80 Vincent Square
London SW1P 2PE
Tel: 0845 260 5000
Gardening advice for RHS
members: 0845 260 8000
www.rhs.org.uk
Provides advice and a gardener's
calendar, as well as information on
joining the RHS.

The Herb Society
Sulgrave Manor
Sulgrave
Banbury
Oxfordshire OX17 2SD
Tel: 0845 491 8699/01295 768899
www.herbsociety.co.uk

The National Vegetable Society
www.nvsuk.org.uk
Various articles on growing
vegetables, fruit and herbs, plus
information on growing vegetables
for shows.

The Organic Gardener
www.the-organic-gardener.com
Explains organic gardening, how to
use gardening tools effectively,
organic weed control, compost
gardening and more.

The Soil Association
South Plaza
Marlborough Street
Bristol BS1 3NX
Tel: 0117 314 5000
www.soilassociation.org
The UK's leading environmental
charity promoting sustainable,
organic farming.
See also: www.whyorganic.org
Consumer website from The Soil
Association providing information
on organic issues.

Town and City Gardens
Part of The FreeTime Web Group
7 Borthwick Place
Balmullo
Fife KY16 0EB
www.gardening-centre.co.uk
Information and an online shop.

Vegetable Garden
www.vegetable-gardens.co.uk
Vegetable growing guides and a
forum to ask for advice from other
gardeners.

Vegetable Plants Direct
Sparra Park Cottage
Upper Tamar Lake
Bude
Cornwall EX23 9SB
Tel: 01288 321175
www.vegetableplantsdirect.co.uk
Mail-order company with a choice
of organically grown (grown from
organic seed, but not in peat-free
compost) and non-organic plants,
and plants suitable for containers,
small gardens and allotments.

www.keirg.freeserve.co.uk/diary/
Growing vegetables on an
allotment – an allotment diary.

Seed suppliers

Association Kokopelli
www.terredesemences.com
contactus@organicseedsonline.com
'The Seeds of Kokopelli' lists 1,000
varieties of organic seeds available
to purchase online.

Beans and Herbs
The Herbary
161 Chapel Street
Horningsham
Warminster
Wiltshire BA12 7LU
www.beansandherbs.co.uk

Chiltern Seeds
Bortree Stile
Ulverston
Cumbria LA12 7PB
www.chilternseeds.co.uk

Dobies of Devon
Long Road
Paignton
Devon TQ4 7SX
Tel: 0844 701 7623
www.dobies.co.uk

D.T. Brown
Bury Road
Newmarket CB8 7QB
Tel: 0845 371 0532
www.dtbrownseeds.co.uk

Garden Seeds UK
6 Elmwood Avenue
Bognor Regis
West Sussex. PO22 8DE
Tel: 01243 829584
www.gardenseeds.co.uk

Harrod Horticultural
Pinbush Road
Lowestoft
Suffolk NR33 7NL
Tel: 0845 218 5301
www.harrodhorticultural.com
Equipment and organic seeds.

MAS Seed Specialists
4 Pinhills
Wenhill Heights
Calne
Wiltshire SN11 OSA
Tel: 01249 819013
www.meadowmania.co.uk

Mr Fothergill's
Kentford
Suffolk CB8 7QB
Tel: 0845 371 0518
www.mr-fothergills.co.uk

Nicky's Nursery
33 Fairfield Road
Broadstairs
Kent CT10 2JU
Tel: 01843 600972
www.nickys-nursery.co.uk

Secret Seeds
Cove
Tiverton
Devon EX16 7RU
Tel: 01398 331946
www.secretseeds.com

Suttons
Woodview Road
Paignton
Devon TQ4 7NG
Tel: 0844 922 0606
www.suttons.co.uk

Tamar Organics
Cartha Martha Farm
Rezare
Launceston
Cornwall PL15 9NX
Tel: 01579 371087
sales@tamarorganics.com

**The Organic Gardening
Catalogue**
Riverdene Business Park
Molesey Road
Hersham
Surrey KT12 4RG
Tel: 0845 130 1304

www.organiccatalog.com
The official catalogue of Garden
Organic (HDRA).

The Real Seed Catalogue
Brithdir Mawr Farm
Newport near Fishguard
Pembrokeshire SA42 0QJ
Tel: 01239 821107
www.realseeds.co.uk
info@realseeds.co.uk

Seeds of Italy
C3 Phoenix Industrial Estate
Rosslyn Crescent
Harrow
Middlesex HA1 2SP
Tel: 0208 427 5020
www.seedsofitaly.com

Suffolk Herbs
Monks Farm
Kelvedon
Colchester
Essex CO5 9PG
Tel: 01376 572456
www.suffolkherbs.com

Thompson & Morgan
www.thompson-morgan.com
Email: ccare@thompson-
morgan.com
Tel: 0844 2485383

Tuckers Seeds
Brewery Meadow
Stonepark
Ashburton
Newton Abbot
Devon TQ13 7DG
Tel: 01364 652233
www.tuckers-seeds.co.uk

Unwins
Mail Order Department
Alconbury Hill
Huntingdon PE28 4HY
Tel: 01480 443395
www.unwins.co.uk

Index